Walt Disney's Donald Duck

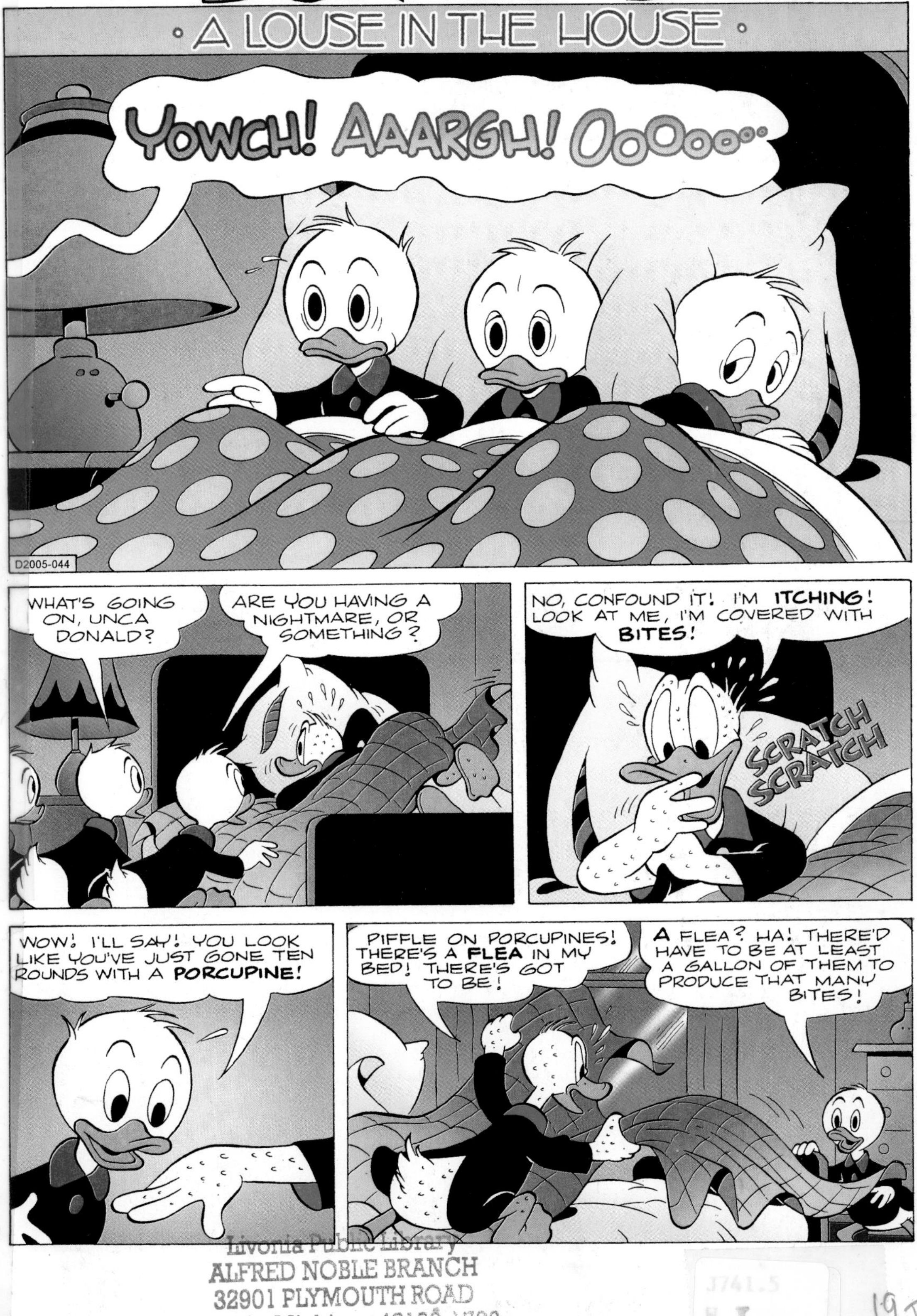
A LOUSE IN THE HOUSE
YOWCH! AAARGH! OoOoo••
D2005-044
WHAT'S GOING ON, UNCA DONALD?
ARE YOU HAVING A NIGHTMARE, OR SOMETHING?
NO, CONFOUND IT! I'M ITCHING! LOOK AT ME, I'M COVERED WITH BITES!
SCRATCH SCRATCH
WOW! I'LL SAY! YOU LOOK LIKE YOU'VE JUST GONE TEN ROUNDS WITH A PORCUPINE!
PIFFLE ON PORCUPINES! THERE'S A FLEA IN MY BED! THERE'S GOT TO BE!
A FLEA? HA! THERE'D HAVE TO BE AT LEAST A GALLON OF THEM TO PRODUCE THAT MANY BITES!

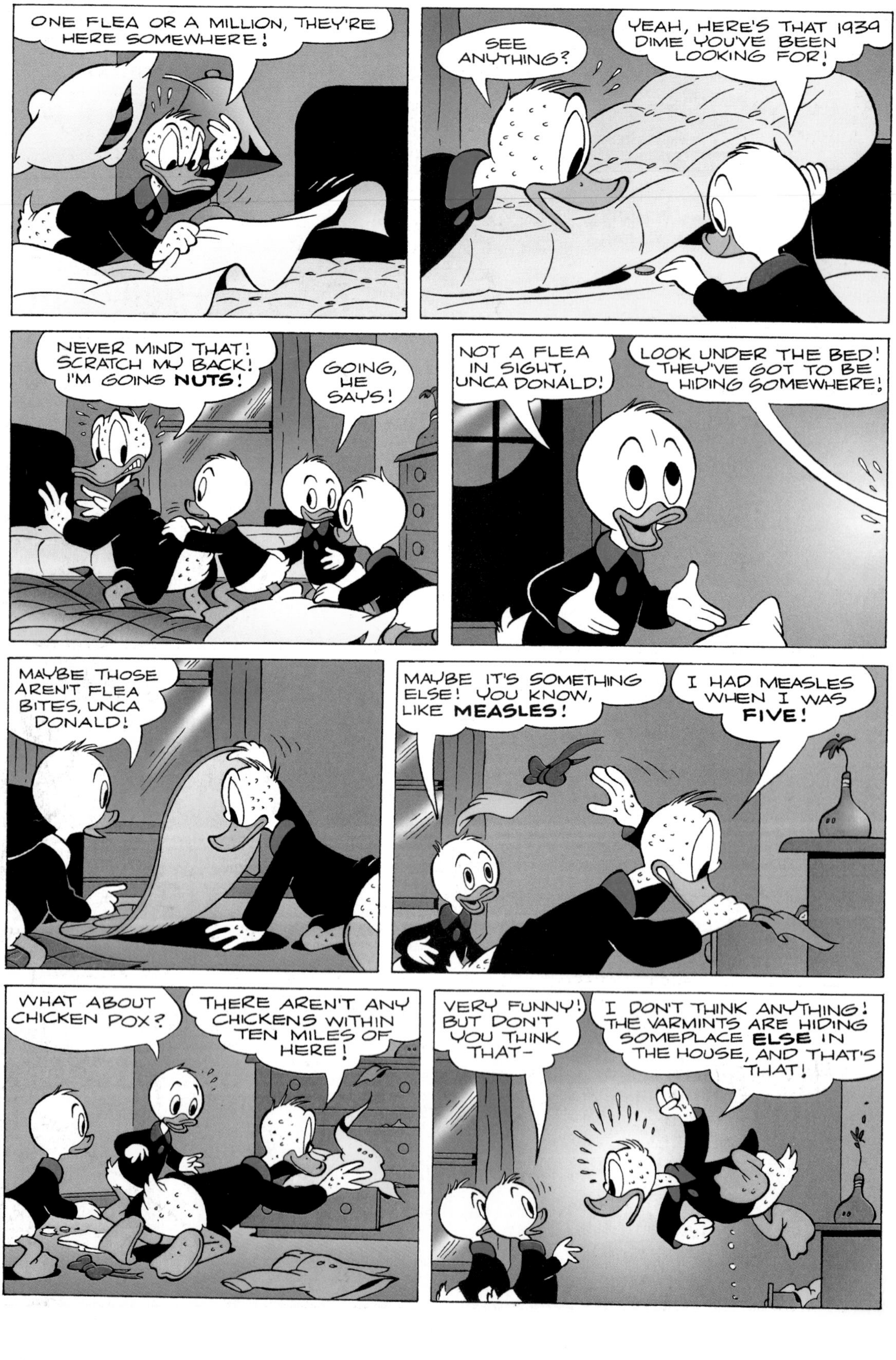
ONE FLEA OR A MILLION, THEY'RE HERE SOMEWHERE!
SEE ANYTHING?
YEAH, HERE'S THAT 1939 DIME YOU'VE BEEN LOOKING FOR!
NEVER MIND THAT! SCRATCH MY BACK! I'M GOING **NUTS**!
GOING, HE SAYS!
NOT A FLEA IN SIGHT, UNCA DONALD!
LOOK UNDER THE BED! THEY'VE GOT TO BE HIDING SOMEWHERE!
MAYBE THOSE AREN'T FLEA BITES, UNCA DONALD!
MAYBE IT'S SOMETHING ELSE! YOU KNOW, LIKE **MEASLES**!
I HAD MEASLES WHEN I WAS **FIVE**!
WHAT ABOUT CHICKEN POX?
THERE AREN'T ANY CHICKENS WITHIN TEN MILES OF HERE!
VERY FUNNY! BUT DON'T YOU THINK THAT-
I DON'T THINK ANYTHING! THE VARMINTS ARE HIDING SOMEPLACE **ELSE** IN THE HOUSE, AND THAT'S THAT!

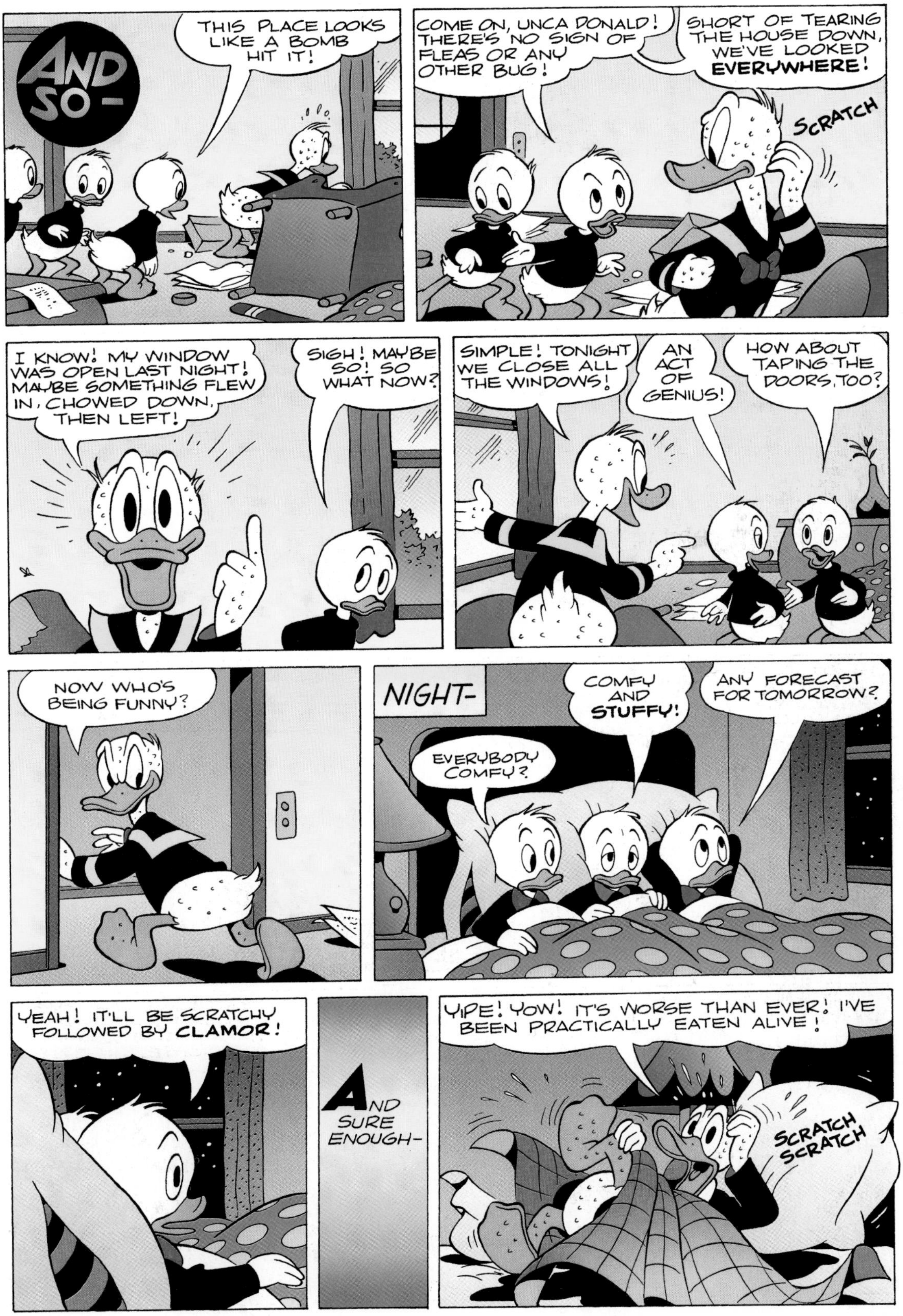
AND SO -
THIS PLACE LOOKS LIKE A BOMB HIT IT!
COME ON, UNCA DONALD! THERE'S NO SIGN OF FLEAS OR ANY OTHER BUG!
SHORT OF TEARING THE HOUSE DOWN, WE'VE LOOKED **EVERYWHERE!**
SCRATCH
I KNOW! MY WINDOW WAS OPEN LAST NIGHT! MAYBE SOMETHING FLEW IN, CHOWED DOWN, THEN LEFT!
SIGH! MAYBE SO! SO WHAT NOW?
SIMPLE! TONIGHT WE CLOSE ALL THE WINDOWS!
AN ACT OF GENIUS!
HOW ABOUT TAPING THE DOORS, TOO?
NOW WHO'S BEING FUNNY?
NIGHT-
EVERYBODY COMFY?
COMFY AND **STUFFY!**
ANY FORECAST FOR TOMORROW?
YEAH! IT'LL BE SCRATCHY FOLLOWED BY **CLAMOR!**
AND SURE ENOUGH-
YIPE! YOW! IT'S WORSE THAN EVER! I'VE BEEN PRACTICALLY EATEN ALIVE!
SCRATCH SCRATCH

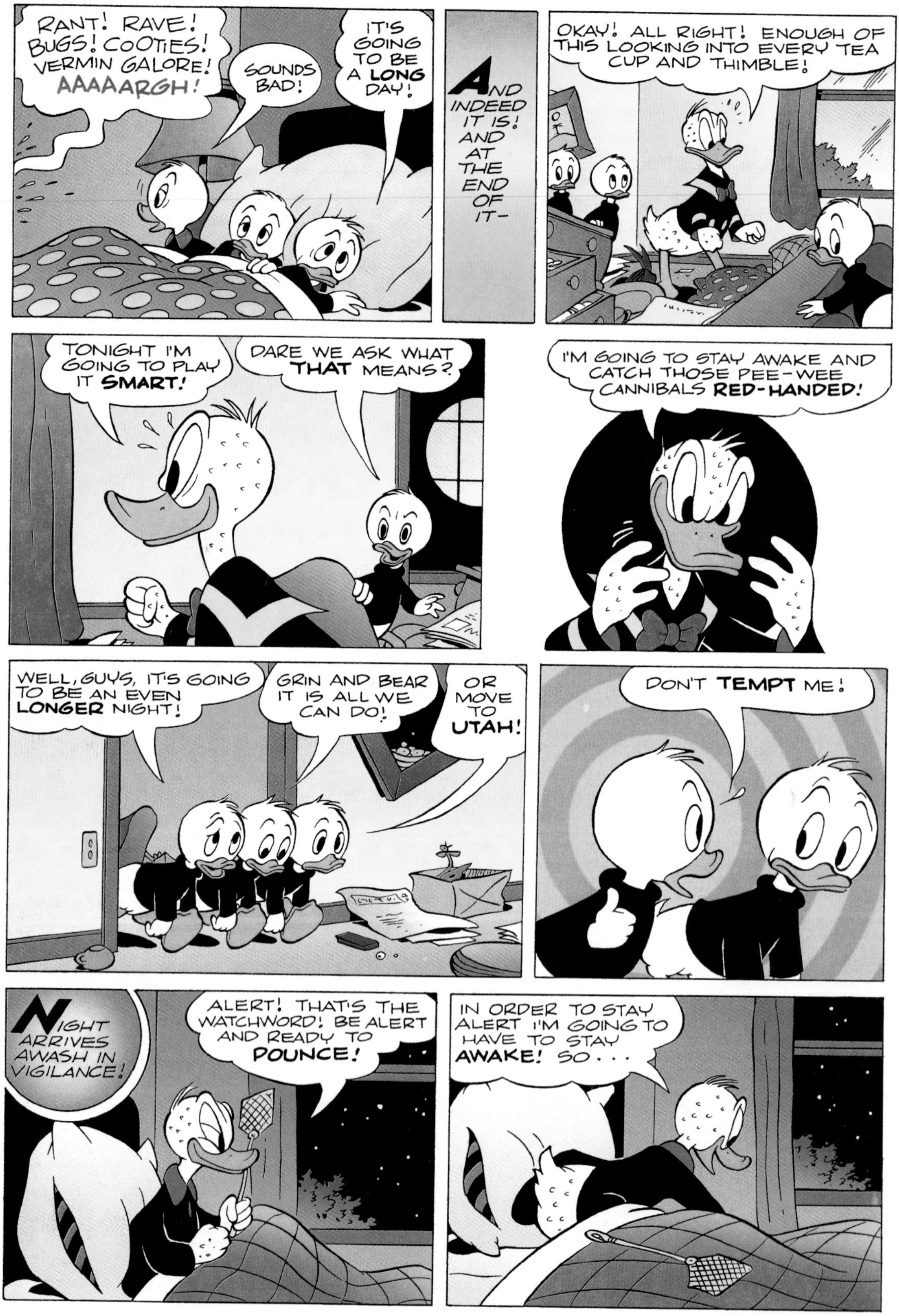
RANT! RAVE! BUGS! COOTIES! VERMIN GALORE! AAAAARGH!
SOUNDS BAD!
IT'S GOING TO BE A LONG DAY!
AND INDEED IT IS! AND AT THE END OF IT–
OKAY! ALL RIGHT! ENOUGH OF THIS LOOKING INTO EVERY TEA CUP AND THIMBLE!
TONIGHT I'M GOING TO PLAY IT SMART!
DARE WE ASK WHAT THAT MEANS?
I'M GOING TO STAY AWAKE AND CATCH THOSE PEE-WEE CANNIBALS RED-HANDED!
WELL, GUYS, IT'S GOING TO BE AN EVEN LONGER NIGHT!
GRIN AND BEAR IT IS ALL WE CAN DO!
OR MOVE TO UTAH!
DON'T TEMPT ME!
NIGHT ARRIVES AWASH IN VIGILANCE!
ALERT! THAT'S THE WATCHWORD! BE ALERT AND READY TO POUNCE!
IN ORDER TO STAY ALERT I'M GOING TO HAVE TO STAY AWAKE! SO . . .

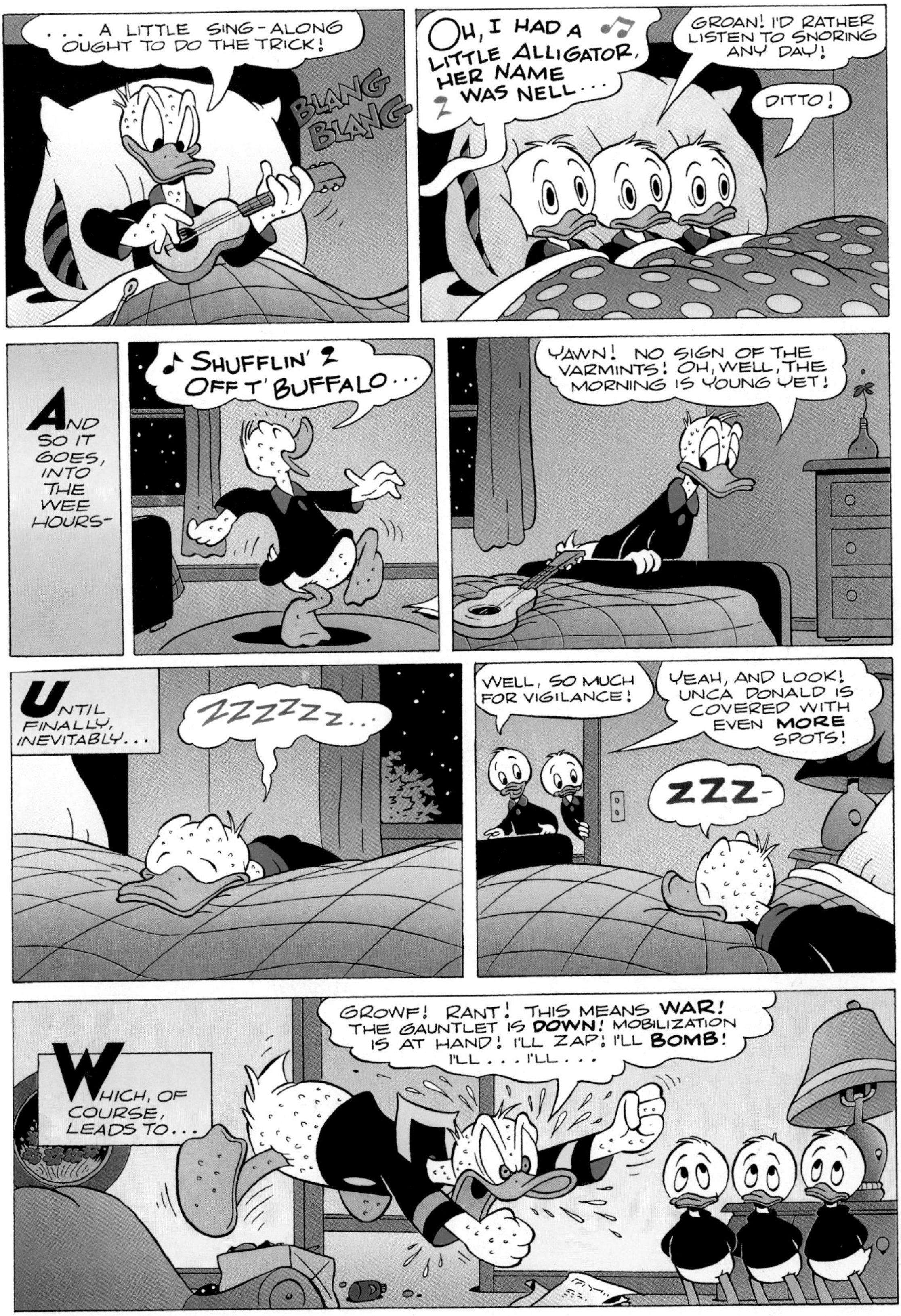
. . . A LITTLE SING-ALONG OUGHT TO DO THE TRICK!
BLANG BLANG
OH, I HAD A LITTLE ALLIGATOR, HER NAME WAS NELL . . .
GROAN! I'D RATHER LISTEN TO SNORING ANY DAY!
DITTO!
AND SO IT GOES, INTO THE WEE HOURS-
SHUFFLIN' OFF T' BUFFALO . . .
YAWN! NO SIGN OF THE VARMINTS! OH, WELL, THE MORNING IS YOUNG YET!
UNTIL FINALLY, INEVITABLY . . .
ZZZZZZz . . .
WELL, SO MUCH FOR VIGILANCE!
YEAH, AND LOOK! UNCA DONALD IS COVERED WITH EVEN **MORE** SPOTS!
ZZZ-
WHICH, OF COURSE, LEADS TO . . .
GROWF! RANT! THIS MEANS **WAR!** THE GAUNTLET IS **DOWN!** MOBILIZATION IS AT HAND! I'LL ZAP! I'LL **BOMB!** I'LL . . . I'LL . . .

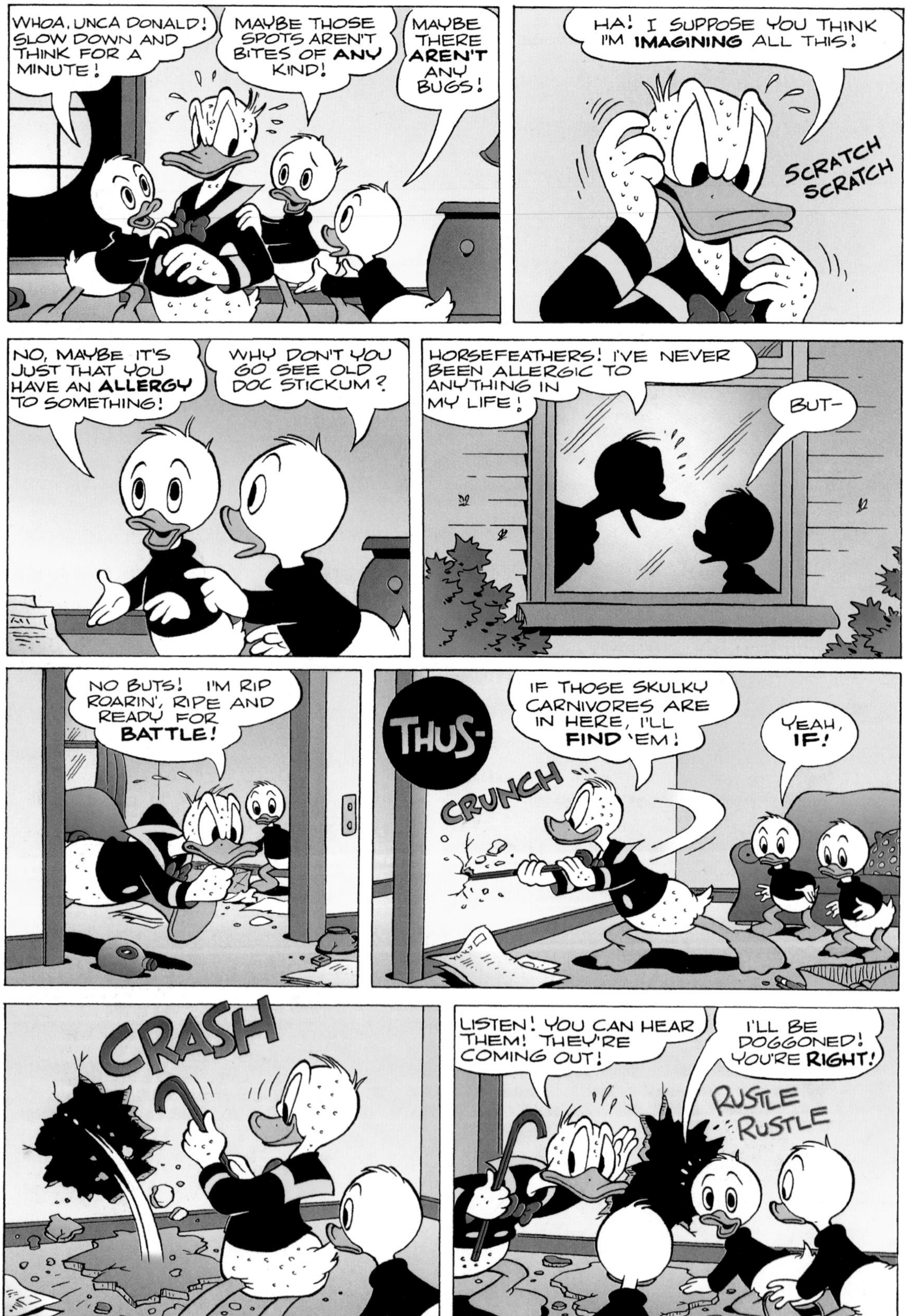
WHOA, UNCA DONALD! SLOW DOWN AND THINK FOR A MINUTE!
MAYBE THOSE SPOTS AREN'T BITES OF ANY KIND!
MAYBE THERE AREN'T ANY BUGS!
HA! I SUPPOSE YOU THINK I'M IMAGINING ALL THIS!
SCRATCH SCRATCH
NO, MAYBE IT'S JUST THAT YOU HAVE AN ALLERGY TO SOMETHING!
WHY DON'T YOU GO SEE OLD DOC STICKUM?
HORSEFEATHERS! I'VE NEVER BEEN ALLERGIC TO ANYTHING IN MY LIFE!
BUT-
NO BUTS! I'M RIP ROARIN', RIPE AND READY FOR BATTLE!
THUS-
IF THOSE SKULKY CARNIVORES ARE IN HERE, I'LL FIND 'EM!
YEAH, IF!
CRUNCH
CRASH
LISTEN! YOU CAN HEAR THEM! THEY'RE COMING OUT!
I'LL BE DOGGONED! YOU'RE RIGHT!
RUSTLE RUSTLE

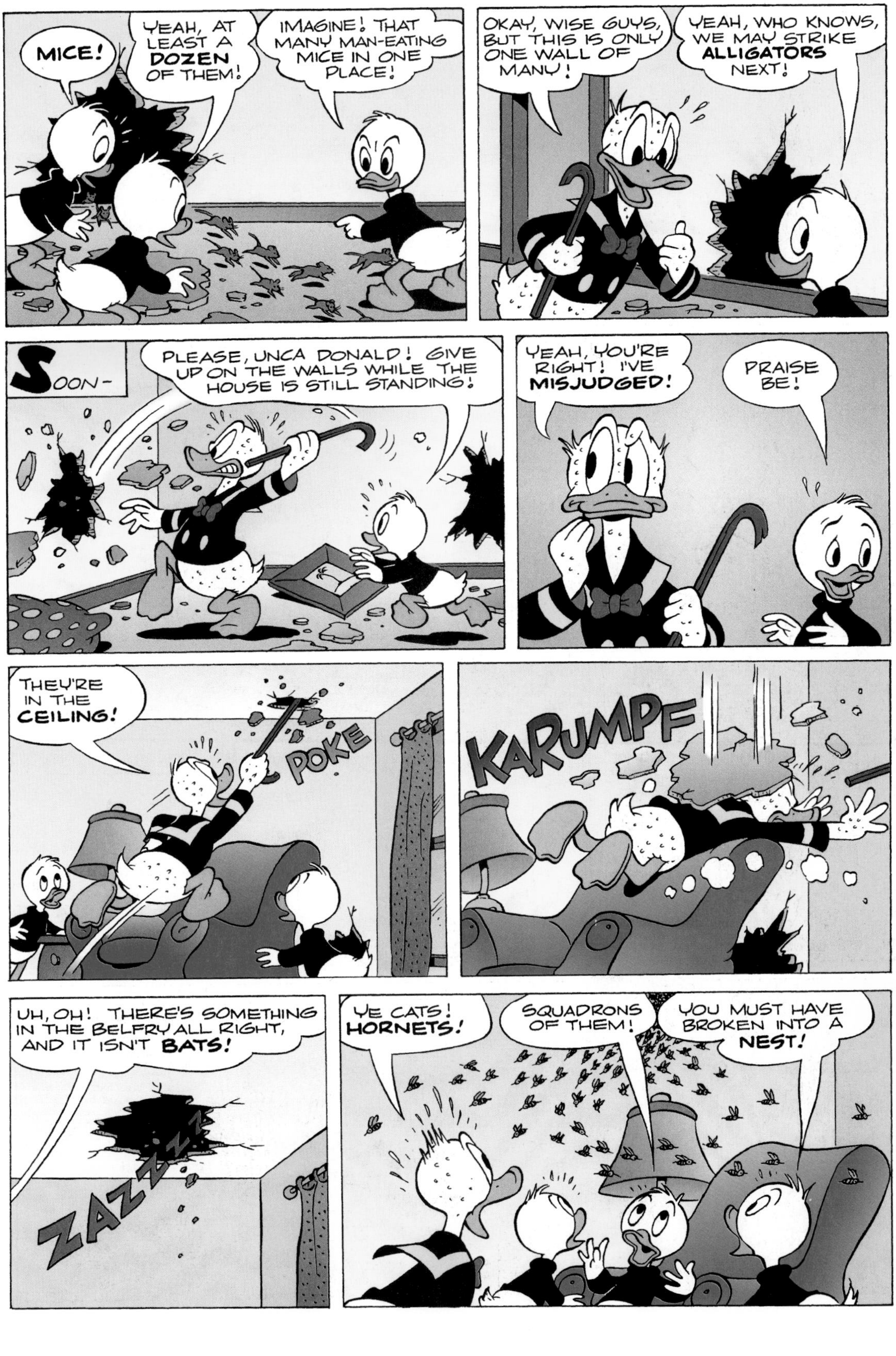
MICE!
YEAH, AT LEAST A DOZEN OF THEM!
IMAGINE! THAT MANY MAN-EATING MICE IN ONE PLACE!
OKAY, WISE GUYS, BUT THIS IS ONLY ONE WALL OF MANY!
YEAH, WHO KNOWS, WE MAY STRIKE ALLIGATORS NEXT!
SOON-
PLEASE, UNCA DONALD! GIVE UP ON THE WALLS WHILE THE HOUSE IS STILL STANDING!
YEAH, YOU'RE RIGHT! I'VE MISJUDGED!
PRAISE BE!
THEY'RE IN THE CEILING!
POKE
KARUMPF
UH, OH! THERE'S SOMETHING IN THE BELFRY ALL RIGHT, AND IT ISN'T BATS!
ZAZZZZZ
YE CATS! HORNETS!
SQUADRONS OF THEM!
YOU MUST HAVE BROKEN INTO A NEST!

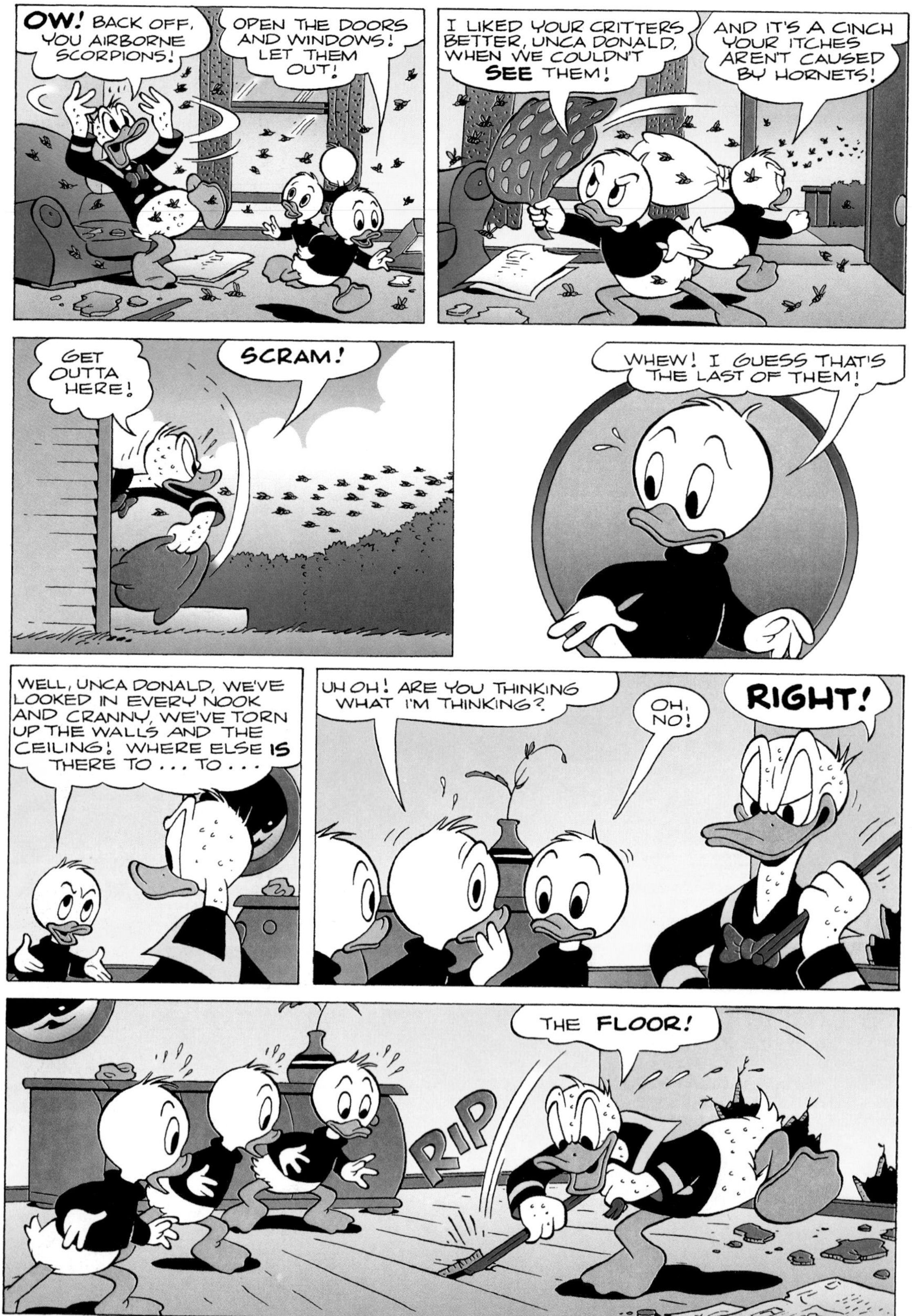
OW! BACK OFF, YOU AIRBORNE SCORPIONS!
OPEN THE DOORS AND WINDOWS! LET THEM OUT!
I LIKED YOUR CRITTERS BETTER, UNCA DONALD, WHEN WE COULDN'T SEE THEM!
AND IT'S A CINCH YOUR ITCHES AREN'T CAUSED BY HORNETS!
GET OUTTA HERE!
SCRAM!
WHEW! I GUESS THAT'S THE LAST OF THEM!
WELL, UNCA DONALD, WE'VE LOOKED IN EVERY NOOK AND CRANNY, WE'VE TORN UP THE WALLS AND THE CEILING! WHERE ELSE IS THERE TO . . . TO . . .
UH OH! ARE YOU THINKING WHAT I'M THINKING?
OH, NO!
RIGHT!
RIP
THE FLOOR!

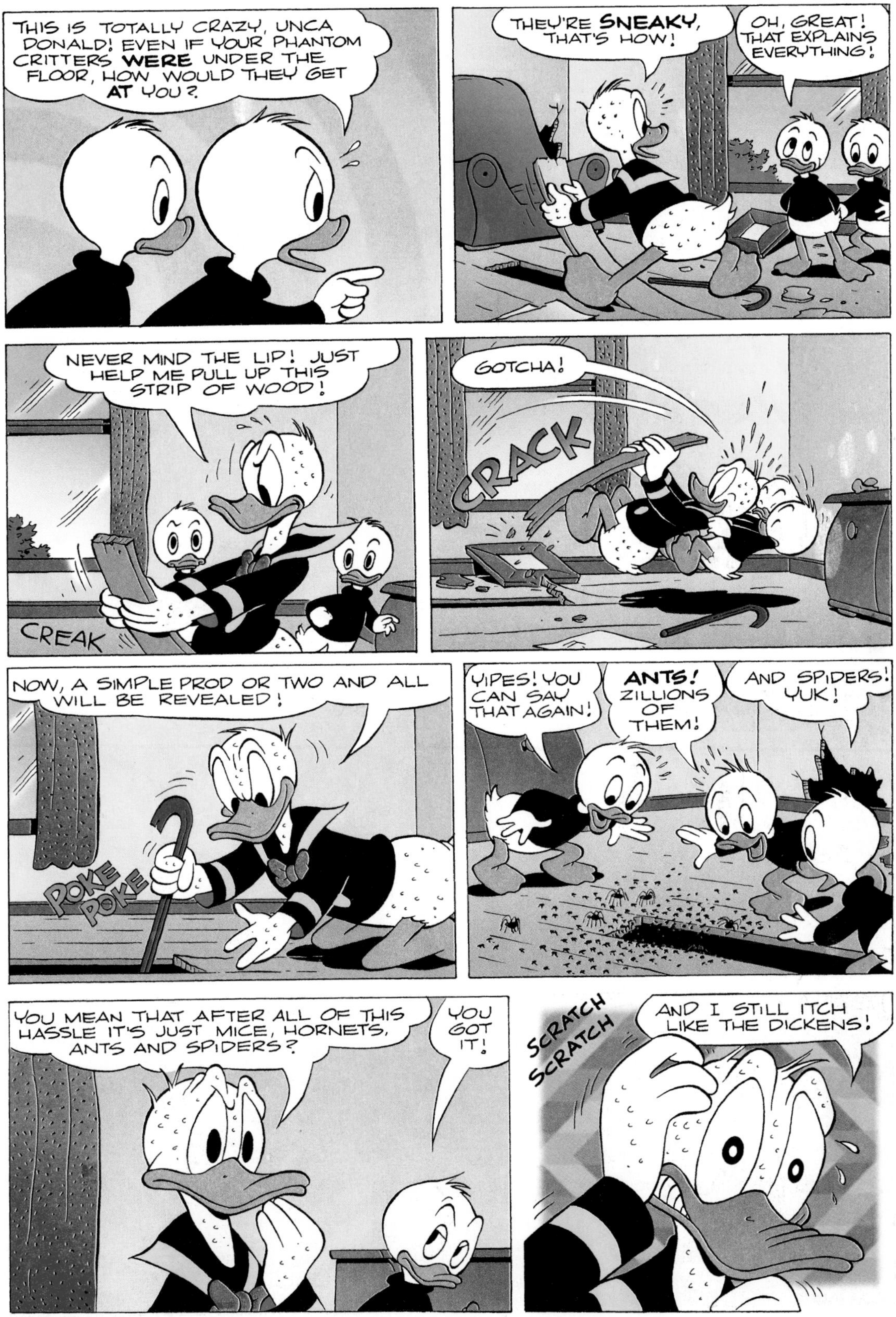
THIS IS TOTALLY CRAZY, UNCA DONALD! EVEN IF YOUR PHANTOM CRITTERS **WERE** UNDER THE FLOOR, HOW WOULD THEY GET **AT** YOU?
THEY'RE **SNEAKY**, THAT'S HOW!
OH, GREAT! THAT EXPLAINS EVERYTHING!
NEVER MIND THE LIP! JUST HELP ME PULL UP THIS STRIP OF WOOD!
CREAK
GOTCHA!
CRACK
NOW, A SIMPLE PROD OR TWO AND ALL WILL BE REVEALED!
POKE POKE
YIPES! YOU CAN SAY THAT AGAIN!
ANTS! ZILLIONS OF THEM!
AND SPIDERS! YUK!
YOU MEAN THAT AFTER ALL OF THIS HASSLE IT'S JUST MICE, HORNETS, ANTS AND SPIDERS?
YOU GOT IT!
SCRATCH SCRATCH
AND I STILL ITCH LIKE THE DICKENS!

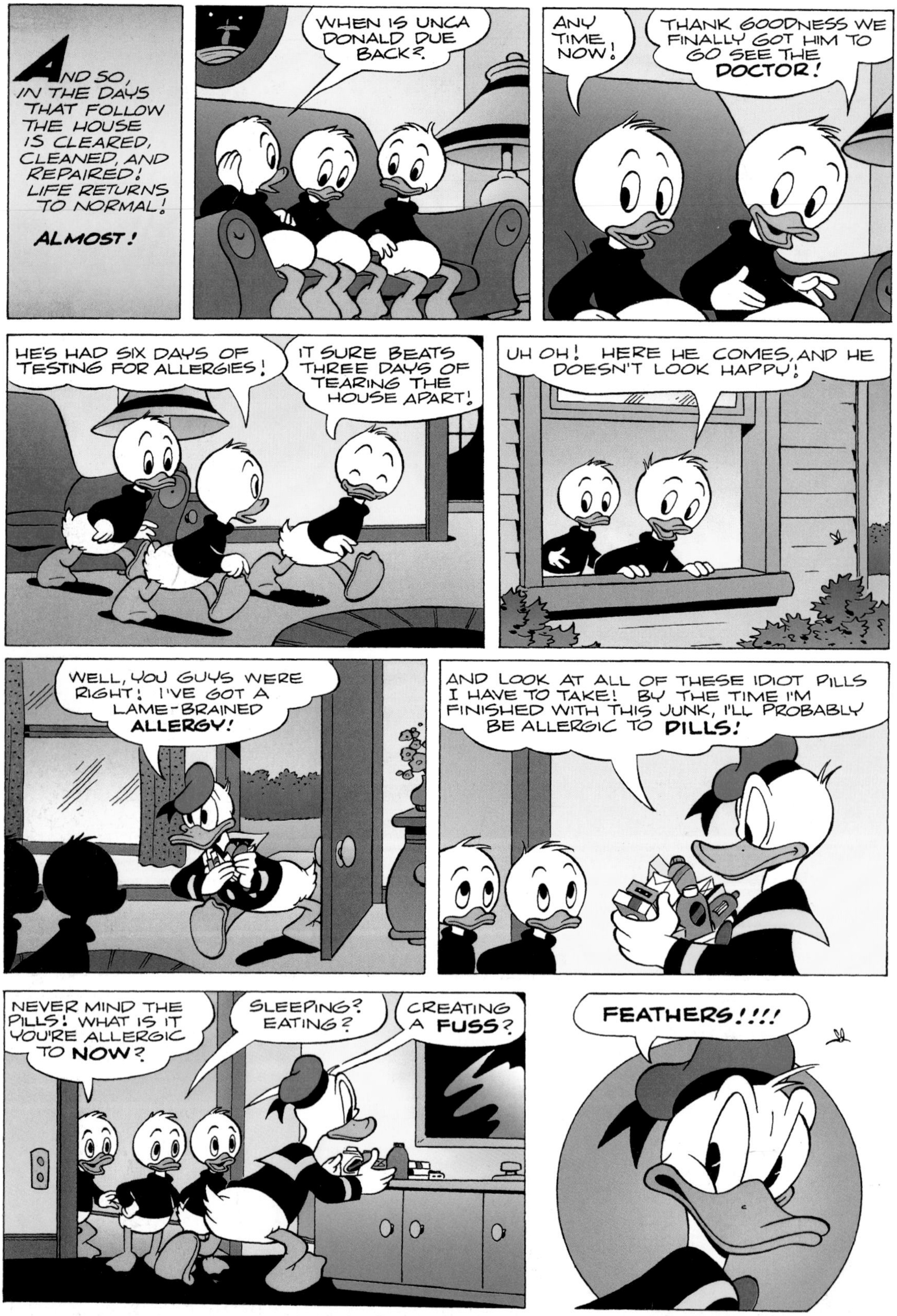
AND SO, IN THE DAYS THAT FOLLOW THE HOUSE IS CLEARED, CLEANED, AND REPAIRED! LIFE RETURNS TO NORMAL!
ALMOST!
WHEN IS UNCA DONALD DUE BACK?
ANY TIME NOW!
THANK GOODNESS WE FINALLY GOT HIM TO GO SEE THE DOCTOR!
HE'S HAD SIX DAYS OF TESTING FOR ALLERGIES!
IT SURE BEATS THREE DAYS OF TEARING THE HOUSE APART!
UH OH! HERE HE COMES, AND HE DOESN'T LOOK HAPPY!
WELL, YOU GUYS WERE RIGHT! I'VE GOT A LAME-BRAINED ALLERGY!
AND LOOK AT ALL OF THESE IDIOT PILLS I HAVE TO TAKE! BY THE TIME I'M FINISHED WITH THIS JUNK, I'LL PROBABLY BE ALLERGIC TO PILLS!
NEVER MIND THE PILLS! WHAT IS IT YOU'RE ALLERGIC TO NOW?
SLEEPING? EATING?
CREATING A FUSS?
FEATHERS!!!!

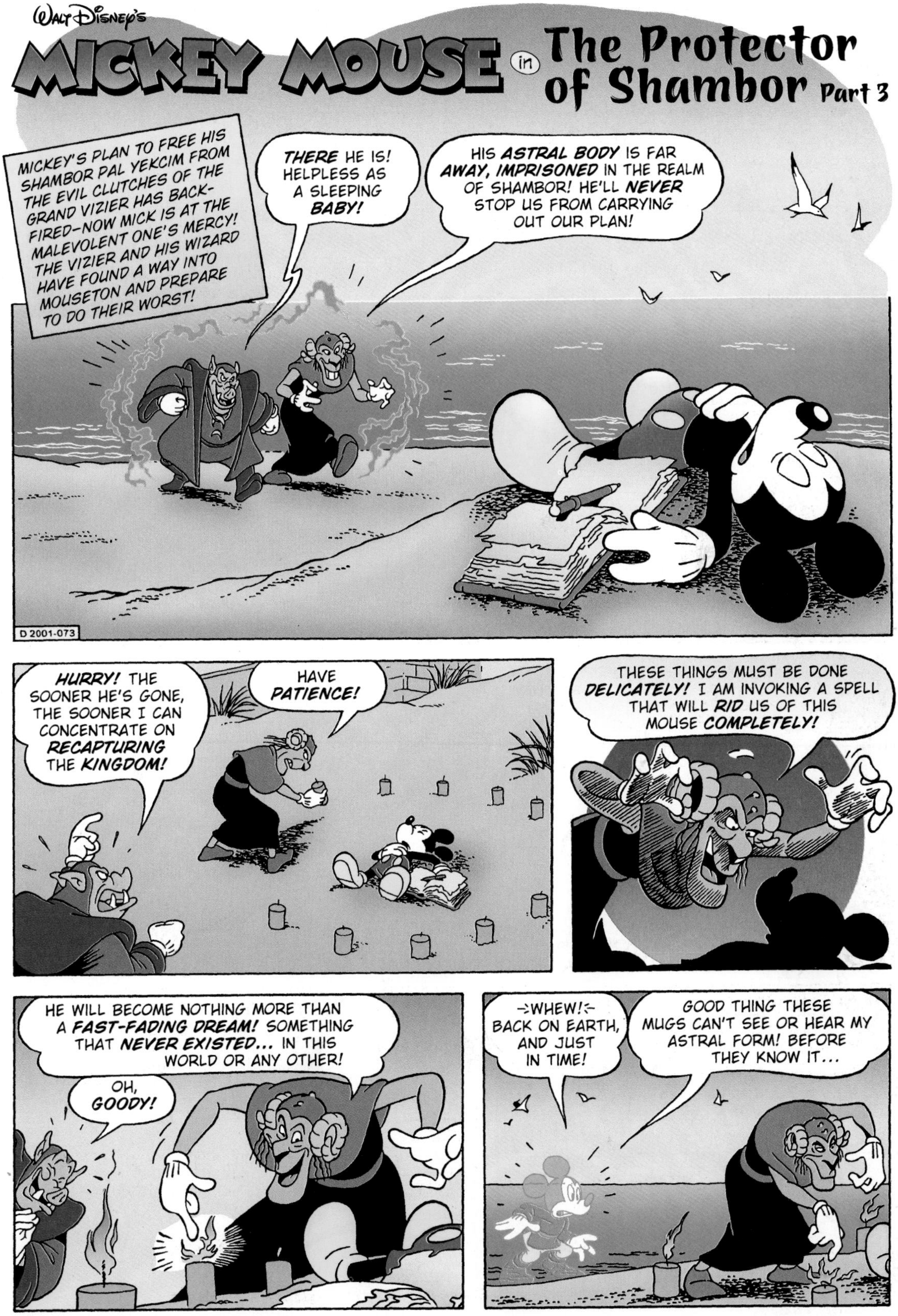
Walt Disney's
MICKEY MOUSE in The Protector of Shambor Part 3
MICKEY'S PLAN TO FREE HIS SHAMBOR PAL YEKCIM FROM THE EVIL CLUTCHES OF THE GRAND VIZIER HAS BACK-FIRED—NOW MICK IS AT THE MALEVOLENT ONE'S MERCY! THE VIZIER AND HIS WIZARD HAVE FOUND A WAY INTO MOUSETON AND PREPARE TO DO THEIR WORST!
THERE HE IS! HELPLESS AS A SLEEPING BABY!
HIS ASTRAL BODY IS FAR AWAY, IMPRISONED IN THE REALM OF SHAMBOR! HE'LL NEVER STOP US FROM CARRYING OUT OUR PLAN!
D 2001-073
HURRY! THE SOONER HE'S GONE, THE SOONER I CAN CONCENTRATE ON RECAPTURING THE KINGDOM!
HAVE PATIENCE!
THESE THINGS MUST BE DONE DELICATELY! I AM INVOKING A SPELL THAT WILL RID US OF THIS MOUSE COMPLETELY!
HE WILL BECOME NOTHING MORE THAN A FAST-FADING DREAM! SOMETHING THAT NEVER EXISTED... IN THIS WORLD OR ANY OTHER!
OH, GOODY!
WHEW! BACK ON EARTH, AND JUST IN TIME!
GOOD THING THESE MUGS CAN'T SEE OR HEAR MY ASTRAL FORM! BEFORE THEY KNOW IT...

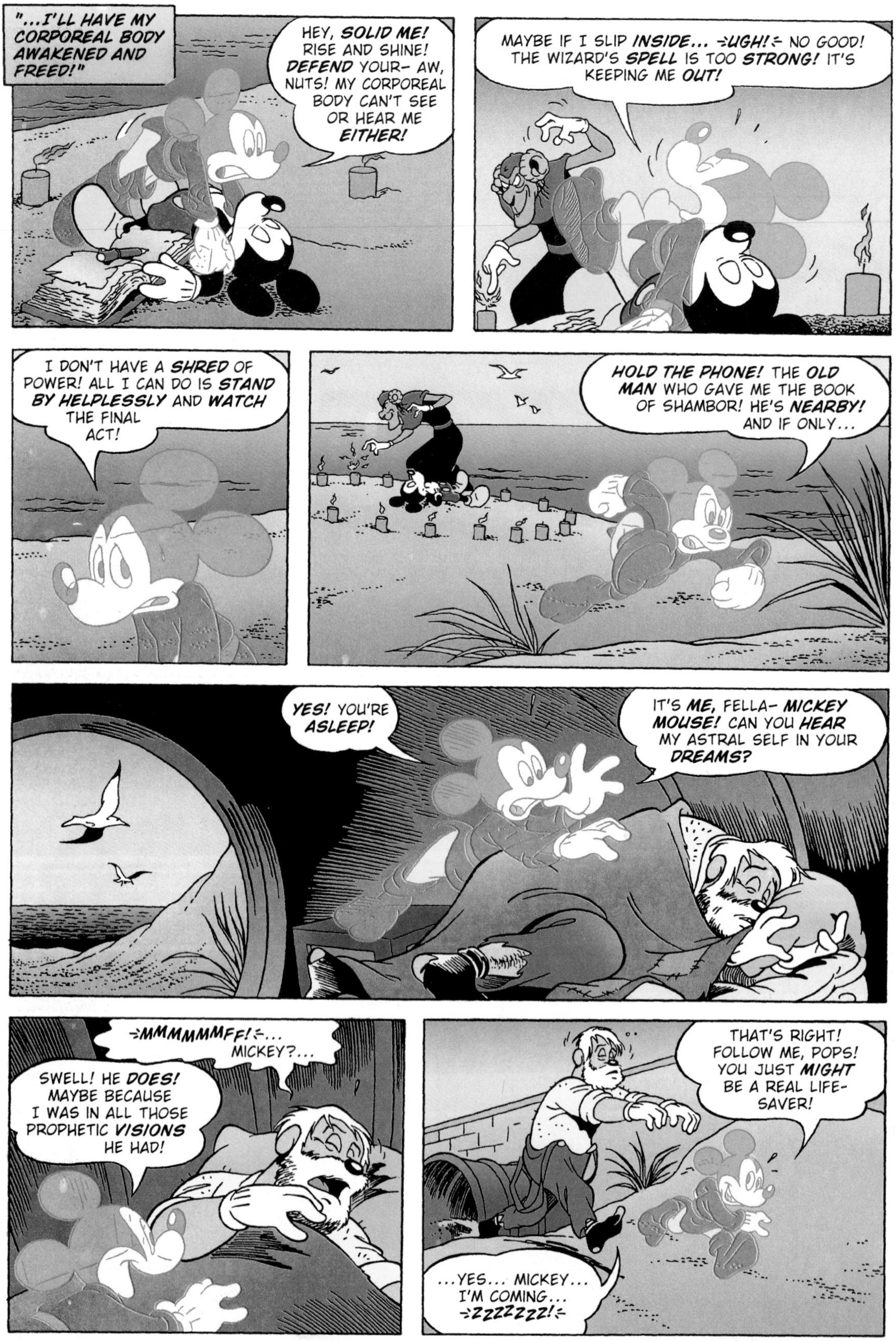
"...I'LL HAVE MY CORPOREAL BODY AWAKENED AND FREED!"
HEY, SOLID ME! RISE AND SHINE! DEFEND YOUR- AW, NUTS! MY CORPOREAL BODY CAN'T SEE OR HEAR ME EITHER!
MAYBE IF I SLIP INSIDE... UGH! NO GOOD! THE WIZARD'S SPELL IS TOO STRONG! IT'S KEEPING ME OUT!
I DON'T HAVE A SHRED OF POWER! ALL I CAN DO IS STAND BY HELPLESSLY AND WATCH THE FINAL ACT!
HOLD THE PHONE! THE OLD MAN WHO GAVE ME THE BOOK OF SHAMBOR! HE'S NEARBY! AND IF ONLY...
YES! YOU'RE ASLEEP!
IT'S ME, FELLA- MICKEY MOUSE! CAN YOU HEAR MY ASTRAL SELF IN YOUR DREAMS?
MMMMMMFF!... MICKEY?...
SWELL! HE DOES! MAYBE BECAUSE I WAS IN ALL THOSE PROPHETIC VISIONS HE HAD!
THAT'S RIGHT! FOLLOW ME, POPS! YOU JUST MIGHT BE A REAL LIFE-SAVER!
...YES... MICKEY... I'M COMING... ZZZZZZZ!

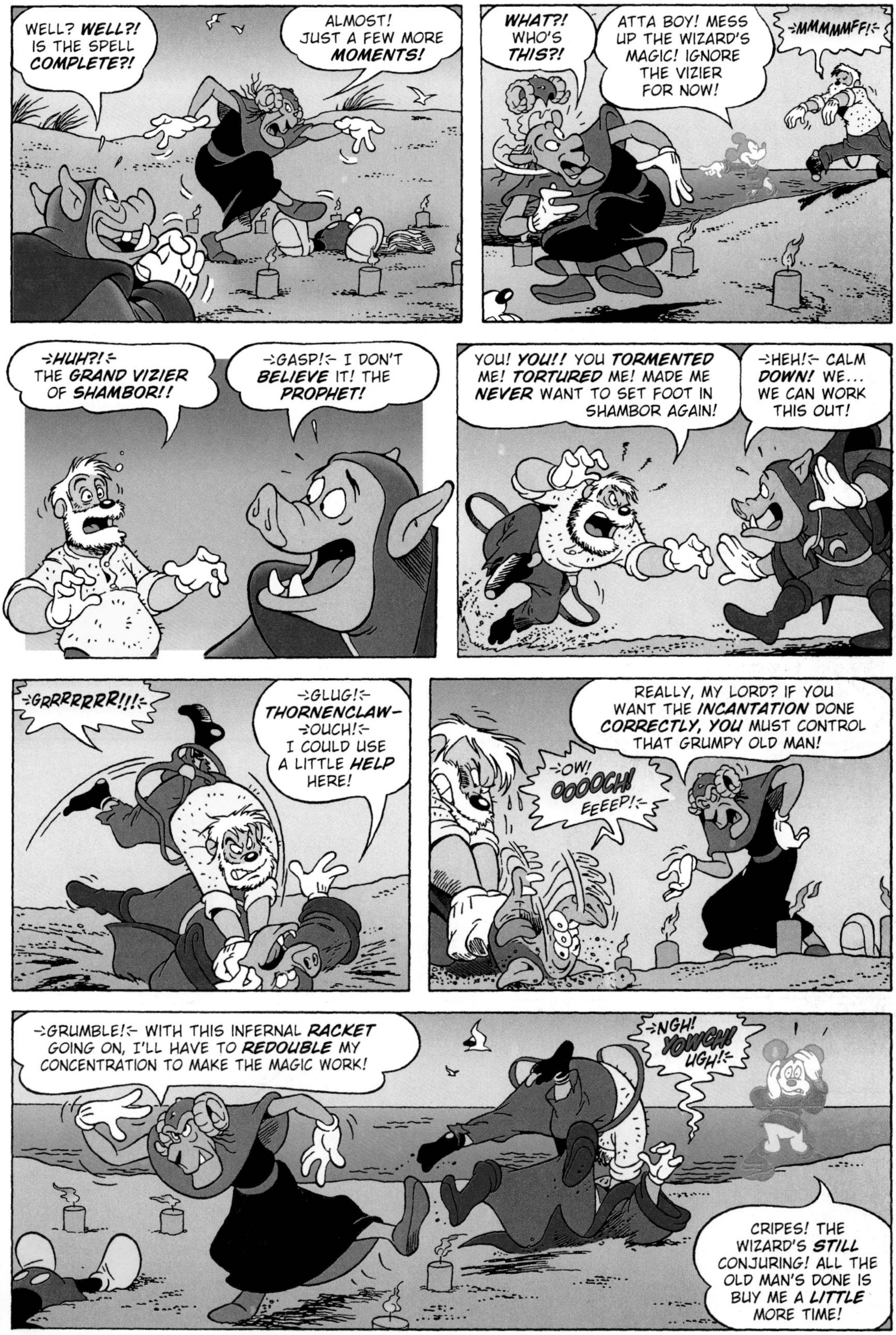
WELL? WELL?! IS THE SPELL COMPLETE?!
ALMOST! JUST A FEW MORE MOMENTS!
WHAT?! WHO'S THIS?!
ATTA BOY! MESS UP THE WIZARD'S MAGIC! IGNORE THE VIZIER FOR NOW!
MMMMMFF!
HUH?! THE GRAND VIZIER OF SHAMBOR!!
GASP! I DON'T BELIEVE IT! THE PROPHET!
YOU! YOU!! YOU TORMENTED ME! TORTURED ME! MADE ME NEVER WANT TO SET FOOT IN SHAMBOR AGAIN!
HEH! CALM DOWN! WE... WE CAN WORK THIS OUT!
GRRRRRRR!!!
GLUG! THORNENCLAW- OUCH! I COULD USE A LITTLE HELP HERE!
REALLY, MY LORD? IF YOU WANT THE INCANTATION DONE CORRECTLY, YOU MUST CONTROL THAT GRUMPY OLD MAN!
OW! OOOOCH! EEEEP!
GRUMBLE! WITH THIS INFERNAL RACKET GOING ON, I'LL HAVE TO REDOUBLE MY CONCENTRATION TO MAKE THE MAGIC WORK!
NGH! YOWCH! UGH!
CRIPES! THE WIZARD'S STILL CONJURING! ALL THE OLD MAN'S DONE IS BUY ME A LITTLE MORE TIME!

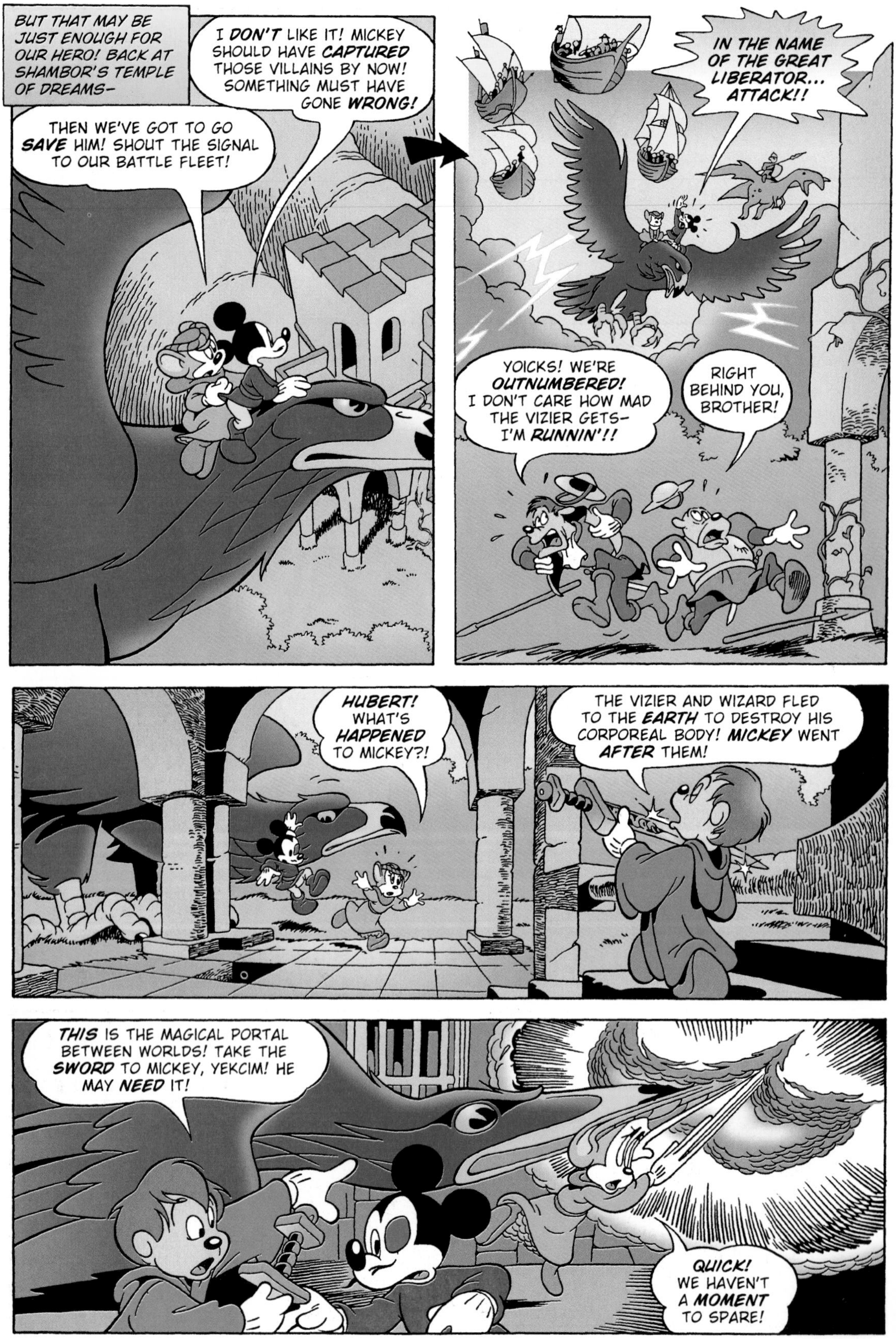
BUT THAT MAY BE JUST ENOUGH FOR OUR HERO! BACK AT SHAMBOR'S TEMPLE OF DREAMS–
I DON'T LIKE IT! MICKEY SHOULD HAVE CAPTURED THOSE VILLAINS BY NOW! SOMETHING MUST HAVE GONE WRONG!
THEN WE'VE GOT TO GO SAVE HIM! SHOUT THE SIGNAL TO OUR BATTLE FLEET!
IN THE NAME OF THE GREAT LIBERATOR... ATTACK!!
YOICKS! WE'RE OUTNUMBERED! I DON'T CARE HOW MAD THE VIZIER GETS– I'M RUNNIN'!!
RIGHT BEHIND YOU, BROTHER!
HUBERT! WHAT'S HAPPENED TO MICKEY?!
THE VIZIER AND WIZARD FLED TO THE EARTH TO DESTROY HIS CORPOREAL BODY! MICKEY WENT AFTER THEM!
THIS IS THE MAGICAL PORTAL BETWEEN WORLDS! TAKE THE SWORD TO MICKEY, YEKCIM! HE MAY NEED IT!
QUICK! WE HAVEN'T A MOMENT TO SPARE!

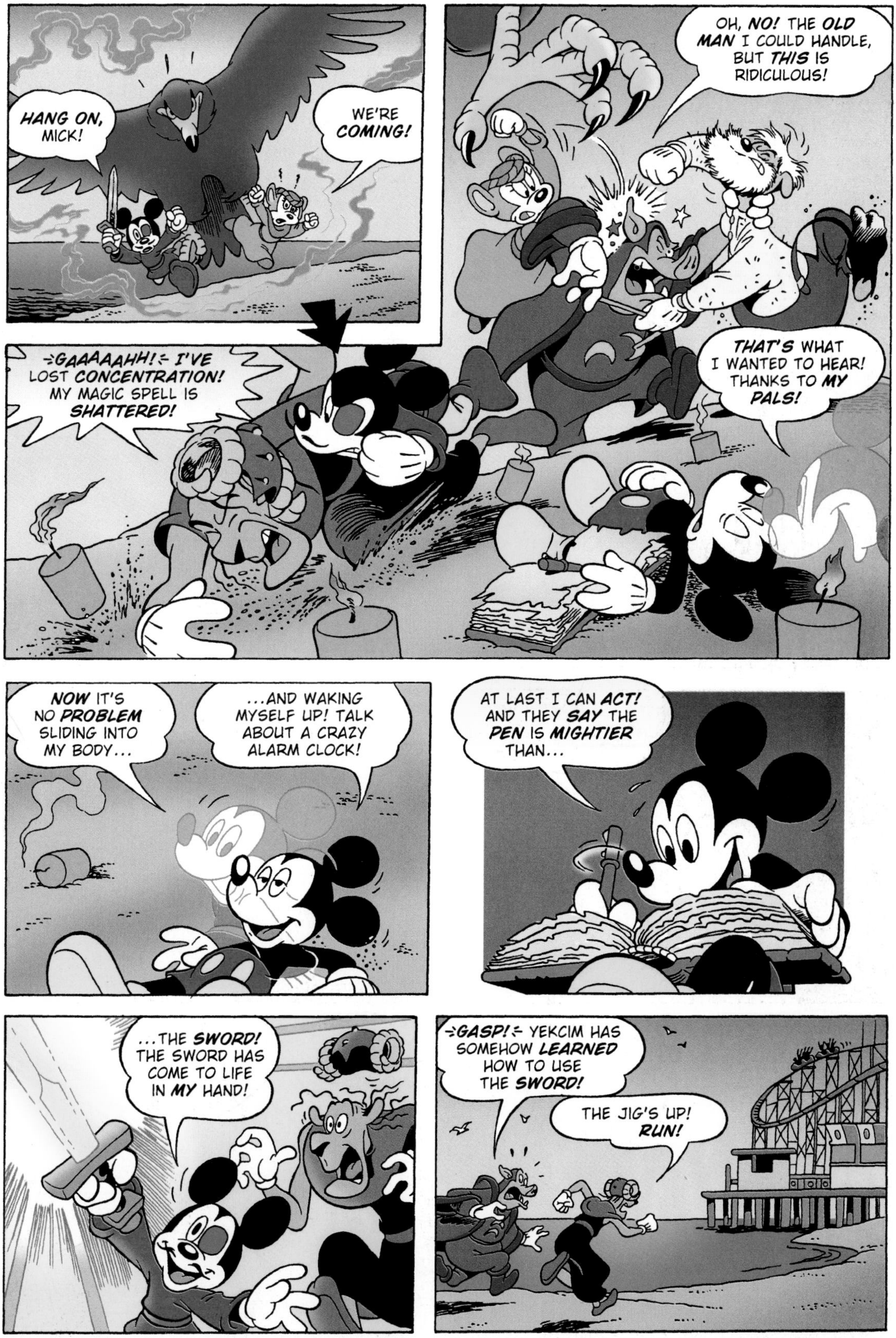
HANG ON, MICK!
WE'RE COMING!
OH, NO! THE OLD MAN I COULD HANDLE, BUT THIS IS RIDICULOUS!
GAAAAAHH! I'VE LOST CONCENTRATION! MY MAGIC SPELL IS SHATTERED!
THAT'S WHAT I WANTED TO HEAR! THANKS TO MY PALS!
NOW IT'S NO PROBLEM SLIDING INTO MY BODY...
...AND WAKING MYSELF UP! TALK ABOUT A CRAZY ALARM CLOCK!
AT LAST I CAN ACT! AND THEY SAY THE PEN IS MIGHTIER THAN...
...THE SWORD! THE SWORD HAS COME TO LIFE IN MY HAND!
GASP! YEKCIM HAS SOMEHOW LEARNED HOW TO USE THE SWORD!
THE JIG'S UP! RUN!

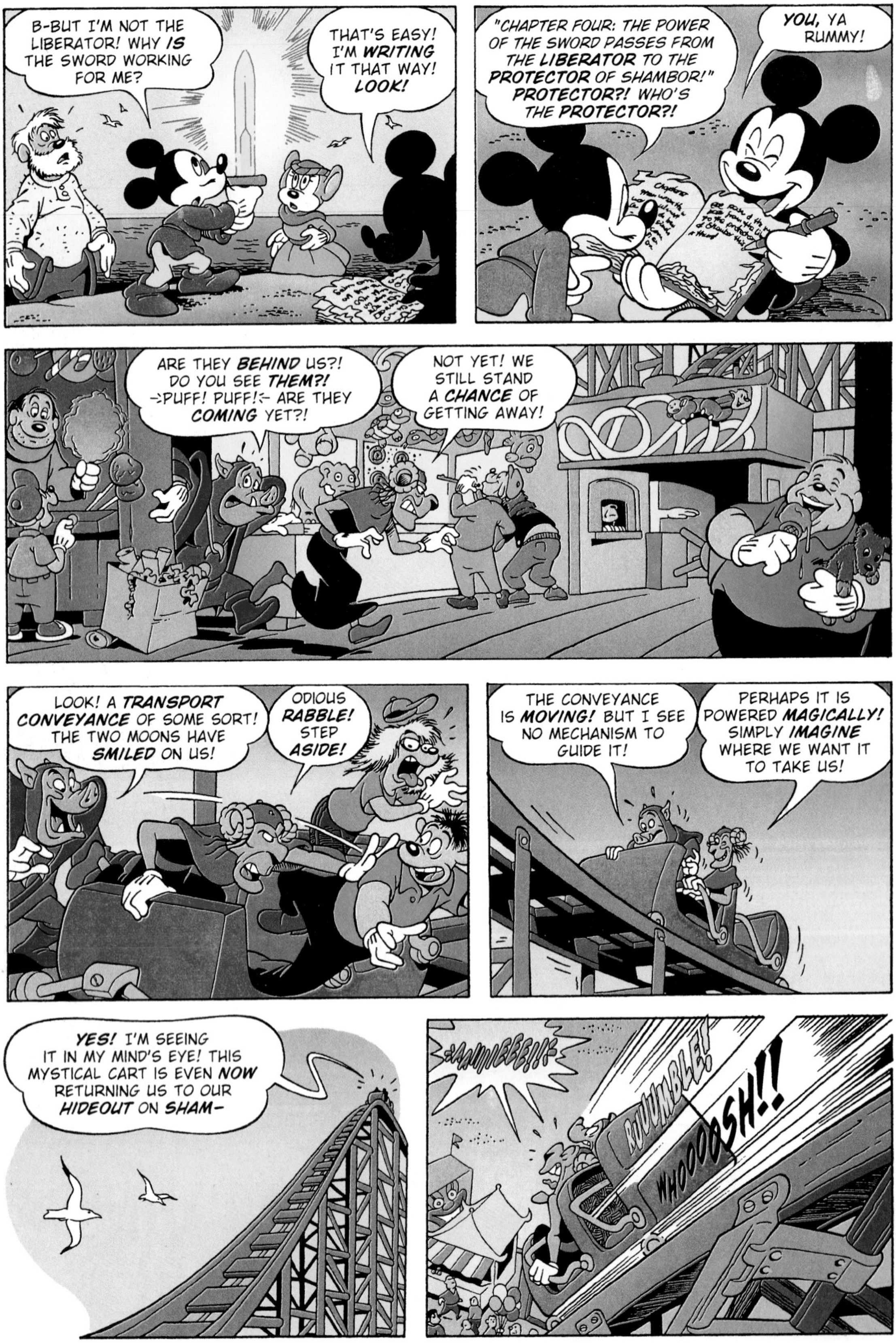

B-BUT I'M NOT THE LIBERATOR! WHY IS THE SWORD WORKING FOR ME?
THAT'S EASY! I'M WRITING IT THAT WAY! LOOK!
"CHAPTER FOUR: THE POWER OF THE SWORD PASSES FROM THE LIBERATOR TO THE PROTECTOR OF SHAMBOR!" PROTECTOR?! WHO'S THE PROTECTOR?!
YOU, YA RUMMY!
ARE THEY BEHIND US?! DO YOU SEE THEM?! -PUFF! PUFF!- ARE THEY COMING YET?!
NOT YET! WE STILL STAND A CHANCE OF GETTING AWAY!
LOOK! A TRANSPORT CONVEYANCE OF SOME SORT! THE TWO MOONS HAVE SMILED ON US!
ODIOUS RABBLE! STEP ASIDE!
THE CONVEYANCE IS MOVING! BUT I SEE NO MECHANISM TO GUIDE IT!
PERHAPS IT IS POWERED MAGICALLY! SIMPLY IMAGINE WHERE WE WANT IT TO TAKE US!
YES! I'M SEEING IT IN MY MIND'S EYE! THIS MYSTICAL CART IS EVEN NOW RETURNING US TO OUR HIDEOUT ON SHAM–
AAAIIIEEEE!!!
RUUUMBLE!
WHOOOOOSH!!

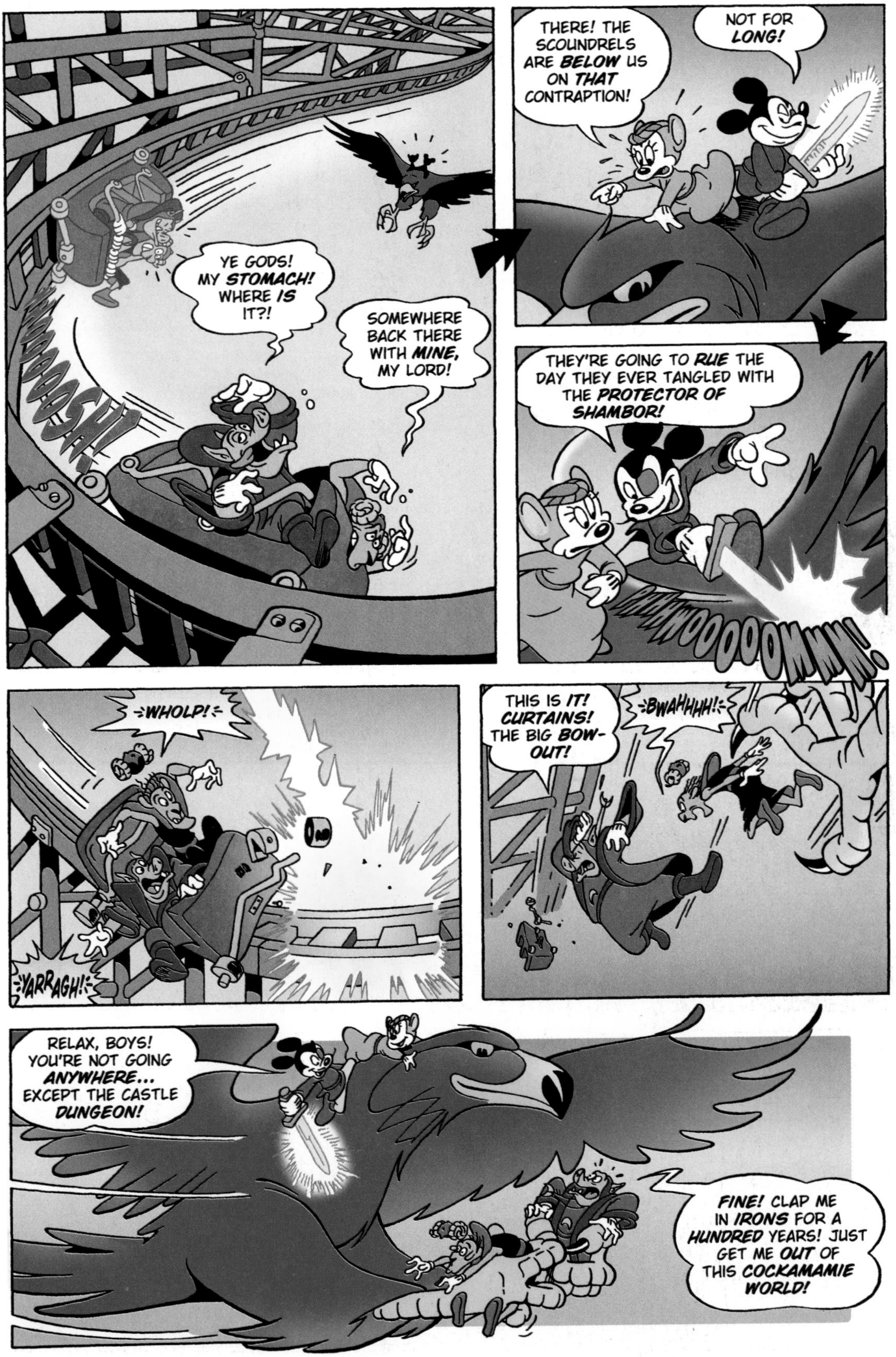

YE GODS! MY STOMACH! WHERE IS IT?!
SOMEWHERE BACK THERE WITH MINE, MY LORD!
THERE! THE SCOUNDRELS ARE BELOW US ON THAT CONTRAPTION!
NOT FOR LONG!
THEY'RE GOING TO RUE THE DAY THEY EVER TANGLED WITH THE PROTECTOR OF SHAMBOR!
-WHOLP!-
-YARRAGH!-
THIS IS IT! CURTAINS! THE BIG BOW-OUT!
-BWAHHHH!-
RELAX, BOYS! YOU'RE NOT GOING ANYWHERE... EXCEPT THE CASTLE DUNGEON!
FINE! CLAP ME IN IRONS FOR A HUNDRED YEARS! JUST GET ME OUT OF THIS COCKAMAMIE WORLD!

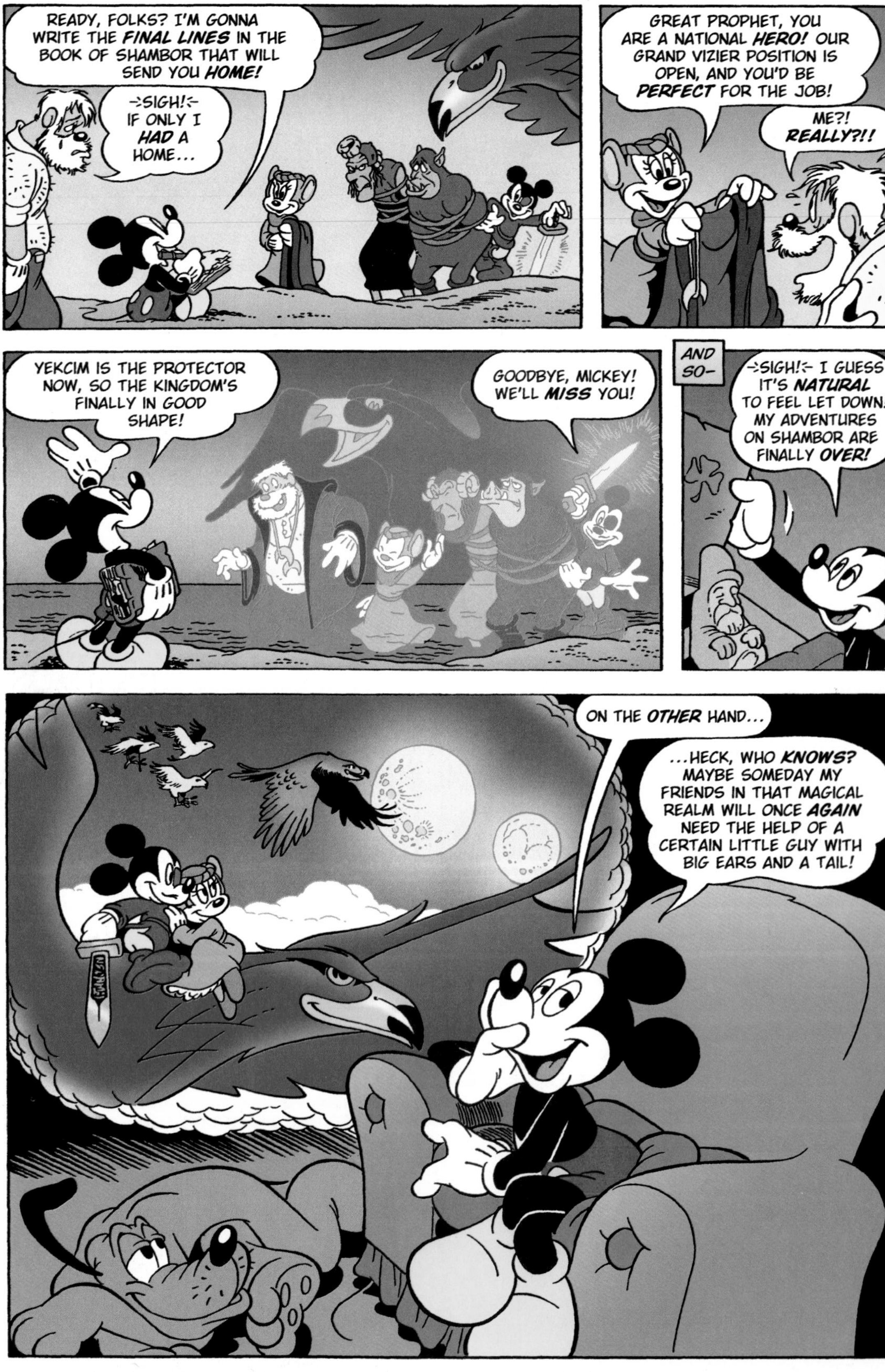
READY, FOLKS? I'M GONNA WRITE THE FINAL LINES IN THE BOOK OF SHAMBOR THAT WILL SEND YOU HOME!
-SIGH!- IF ONLY I HAD A HOME...
GREAT PROPHET, YOU ARE A NATIONAL HERO! OUR GRAND VIZIER POSITION IS OPEN, AND YOU'D BE PERFECT FOR THE JOB!
ME?! REALLY?!!
YEKCIM IS THE PROTECTOR NOW, SO THE KINGDOM'S FINALLY IN GOOD SHAPE!
GOODBYE, MICKEY! WE'LL MISS YOU!
AND SO-
-SIGH!- I GUESS IT'S NATURAL TO FEEL LET DOWN! MY ADVENTURES ON SHAMBOR ARE FINALLY OVER!
ON THE OTHER HAND...
...HECK, WHO KNOWS? MAYBE SOMEDAY MY FRIENDS IN THAT MAGICAL REALM WILL ONCE AGAIN NEED THE HELP OF A CERTAIN LITTLE GUY WITH BIG EARS AND A TAIL!

ULP!

ARE YOU A DONALDIST?

don • ald • ism \ dän'-ld-iz'-em \ *n* : the research of Disney comics, and/or the fan culture that is found among Disney comics aficionados (Jon Gisle, 1973)

Go on, admit it. You like reading about comics history... but you love reading historically important comics themselves. You want a real Disney comics archival book—a thick trade paperback full of those extra-esoteric Duck and Mouse tales that just wouldn't fit in anywhere else.

You're a Donaldist! And we know where you're coming from.

Dive into the 160-page
DISNEY COMICS: 75 YEARS OF INNOVATION *for:*

- *Great Donald sagas by Carl Barks (a newly-restored "Race to the South Seas"), Don Rosa ("Fortune on the Rocks"), and Al Taliaferro (the seminal "Donald's Nephews")*
- *Never-before-reprinted Mickey tales by Floyd Gottfredson ("Mickey Mouse Music") and Romano Scarpa ("AKA Cormorant Number Twelve")*
- *Ducks by Daan Jippes, Dick Kinney, William Van Horn, and Daniel Branca*
- *Mice by Byron Erickson, César Ferioli and Paul Murry*
- *Renato Canini's José Carioca, Gil Turner's Big Bad Wolf—and Brer Rabbit too!*

GEMSTONE PUBLISHING
presents
WALT DISNEY TREASURES VOLUME ONE
Now On Sale

(Any similarity between this book and the Disney DVDs you love to collect is purely intentional!)

WALT DISNEY $12.98
TREASURES
DISNEY COMICS
75 YEARS OF INNOVATION

THE OFFICIAL ANNIVERSARY BOOK

160 PAGES OF COMICS AND FEATURES
INCLUDING STORIES BY FLOYD GOTTFREDSON, CARL BARKS, DON ROSA, ROMANO SCARPA, DAAN JIPPES AND OTHERS
Stories First Published Internationally Between 1930 and 2004

A GEMSTONE LIMITED SERIES
COLLECTING SELECT RARE MATERIAL FOR THE FIRST TIME IN THE USA AND CANADA

© 2007 Disney
Enterprises, Inc.

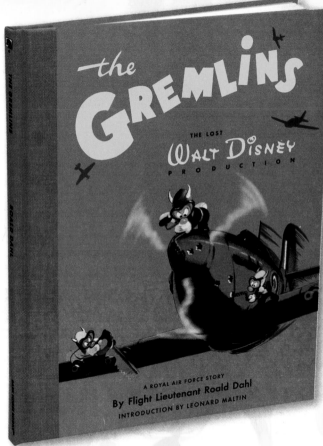

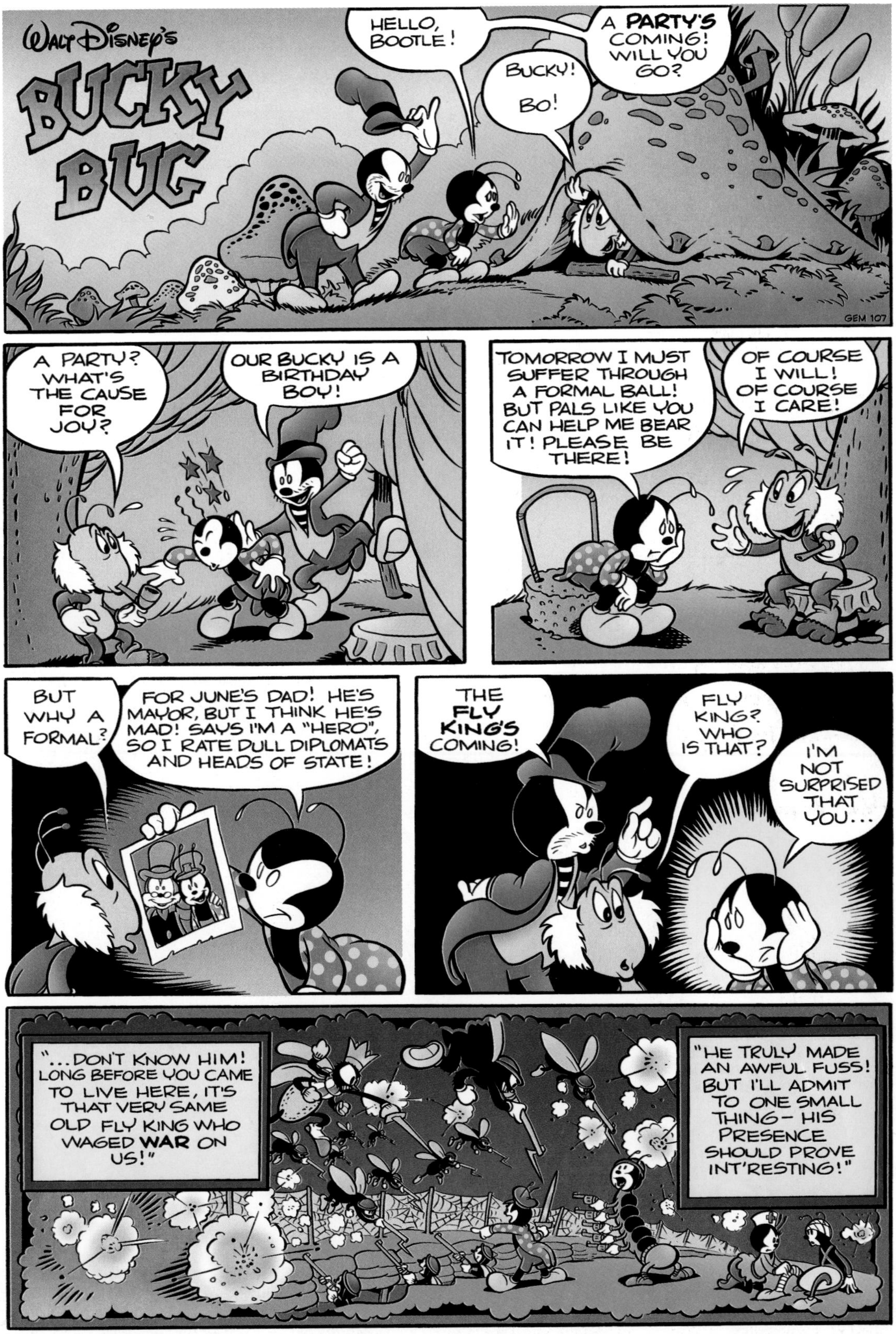
WALT DISNEY'S
BUCKY BUG
HELLO, BOOTLE!
BUCKY! BO!
A PARTY'S COMING! WILL YOU GO?
GEM 107
A PARTY? WHAT'S THE CAUSE FOR JOY?
OUR BUCKY IS A BIRTHDAY BOY!
TOMORROW I MUST SUFFER THROUGH A FORMAL BALL! BUT PALS LIKE YOU CAN HELP ME BEAR IT! PLEASE BE THERE!
OF COURSE I WILL! OF COURSE I CARE!
BUT WHY A FORMAL?
FOR JUNE'S DAD! HE'S MAYOR, BUT I THINK HE'S MAD! SAYS I'M A "HERO", SO I RATE DULL DIPLOMATS AND HEADS OF STATE!
THE FLY KING'S COMING!
FLY KING? WHO IS THAT?
I'M NOT SURPRISED THAT YOU...
"...DON'T KNOW HIM! LONG BEFORE YOU CAME TO LIVE HERE, IT'S THAT VERY SAME OLD FLY KING WHO WAGED WAR ON US!"
"HE TRULY MADE AN AWFUL FUSS! BUT I'LL ADMIT TO ONE SMALL THING— HIS PRESENCE SHOULD PROVE INT'RESTING!"

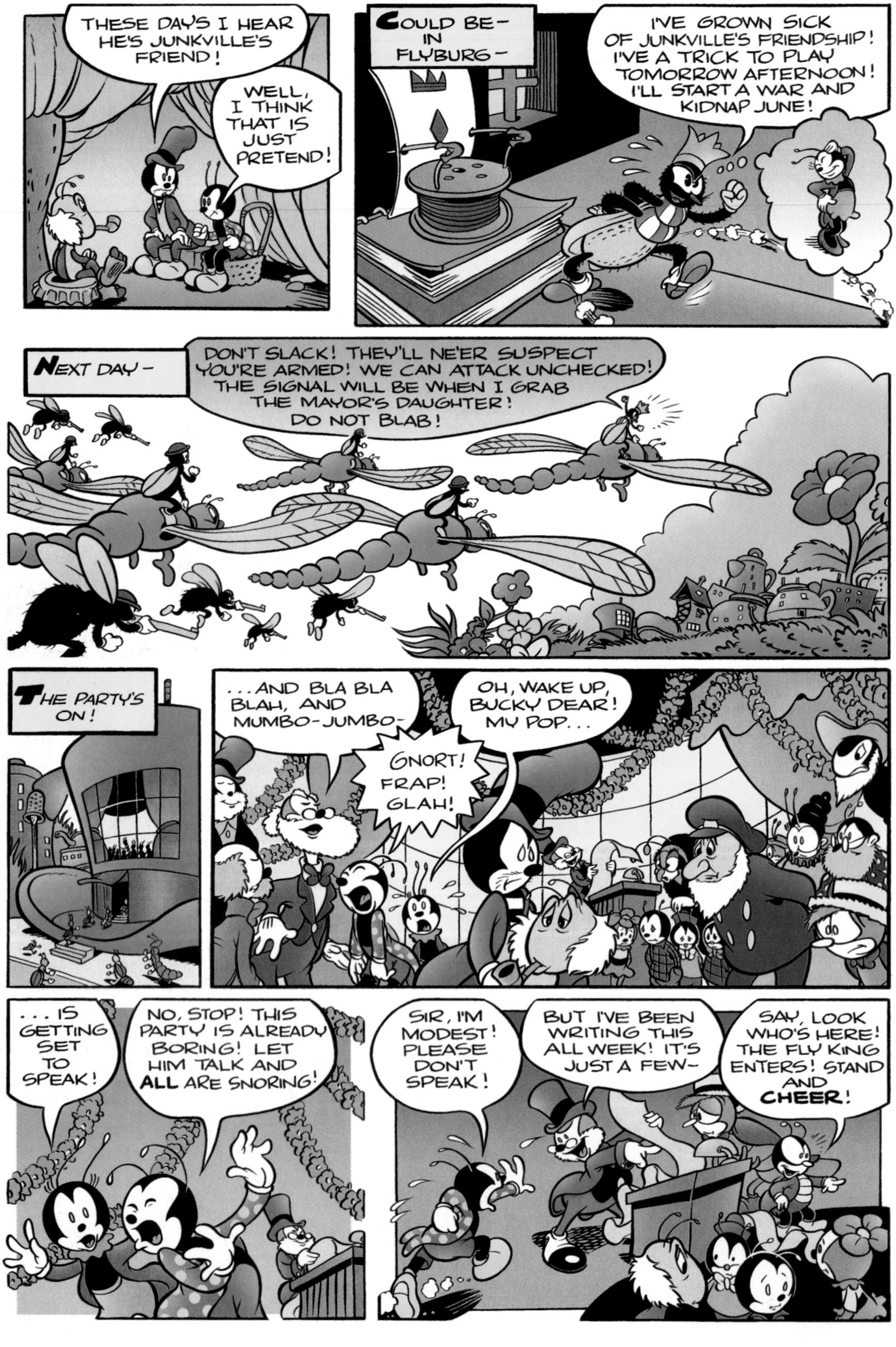
THESE DAYS I HEAR HE'S JUNKVILLE'S FRIEND!
WELL, I THINK THAT IS JUST PRETEND!
COULD BE— IN FLYBURG—
I'VE GROWN SICK OF JUNKVILLE'S FRIENDSHIP! I'VE A TRICK TO PLAY TOMORROW AFTERNOON! I'LL START A WAR AND KIDNAP JUNE!
NEXT DAY—
DON'T SLACK! THEY'LL NE'ER SUSPECT YOU'RE ARMED! WE CAN ATTACK UNCHECKED! THE SIGNAL WILL BE WHEN I GRAB THE MAYOR'S DAUGHTER! DO NOT BLAB!
THE PARTY'S ON!
...AND BLA BLA BLAH, AND MUMBO-JUMBO-
GNORT! FRAP! GLAH!
OH, WAKE UP, BUCKY DEAR! MY POP...
...IS GETTING SET TO SPEAK!
NO, STOP! THIS PARTY IS ALREADY BORING! LET HIM TALK AND ALL ARE SNORING!
SIR, I'M MODEST! PLEASE DON'T SPEAK!
BUT I'VE BEEN WRITING THIS ALL WEEK! IT'S JUST A FEW—
SAY, LOOK WHO'S HERE! THE FLY KING ENTERS! STAND AND CHEER!

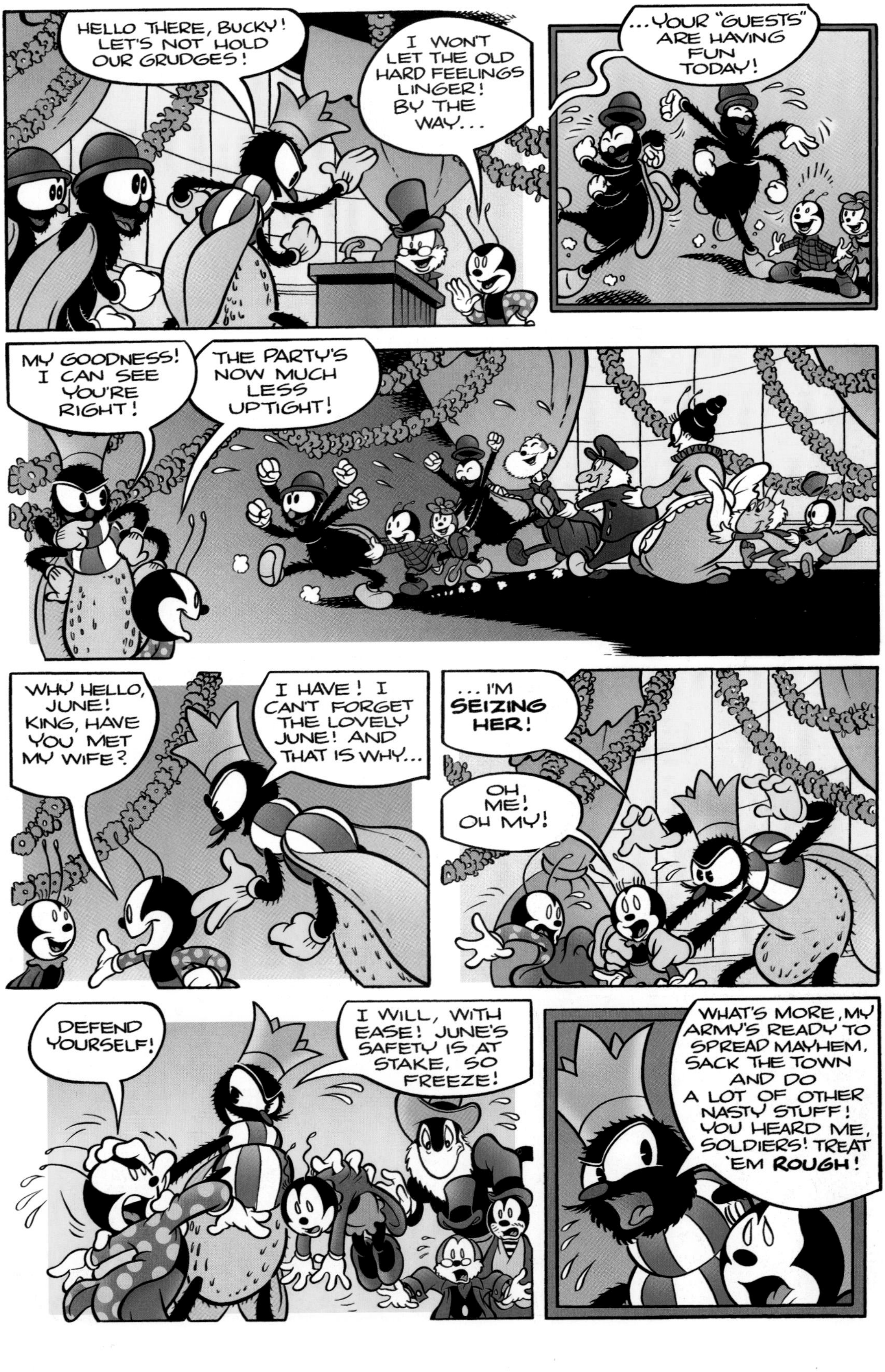
HELLO THERE, BUCKY! LET'S NOT HOLD OUR GRUDGES!
I WON'T LET THE OLD HARD FEELINGS LINGER! BY THE WAY...
...YOUR "GUESTS" ARE HAVING FUN TODAY!
MY GOODNESS! I CAN SEE YOU'RE RIGHT!
THE PARTY'S NOW MUCH LESS UPTIGHT!
WHY HELLO, JUNE! KING, HAVE YOU MET MY WIFE?
I HAVE! I CAN'T FORGET THE LOVELY JUNE! AND THAT IS WHY...
...I'M **SEIZING HER**!
OH ME! OH MY!
DEFEND YOURSELF!
I WILL, WITH EASE! JUNE'S SAFETY IS AT STAKE, SO FREEZE!
WHAT'S MORE, MY ARMY'S READY TO SPREAD MAYHEM, SACK THE TOWN AND DO A LOT OF OTHER NASTY STUFF! YOU HEARD ME, SOLDIERS! TREAT 'EM **ROUGH**!

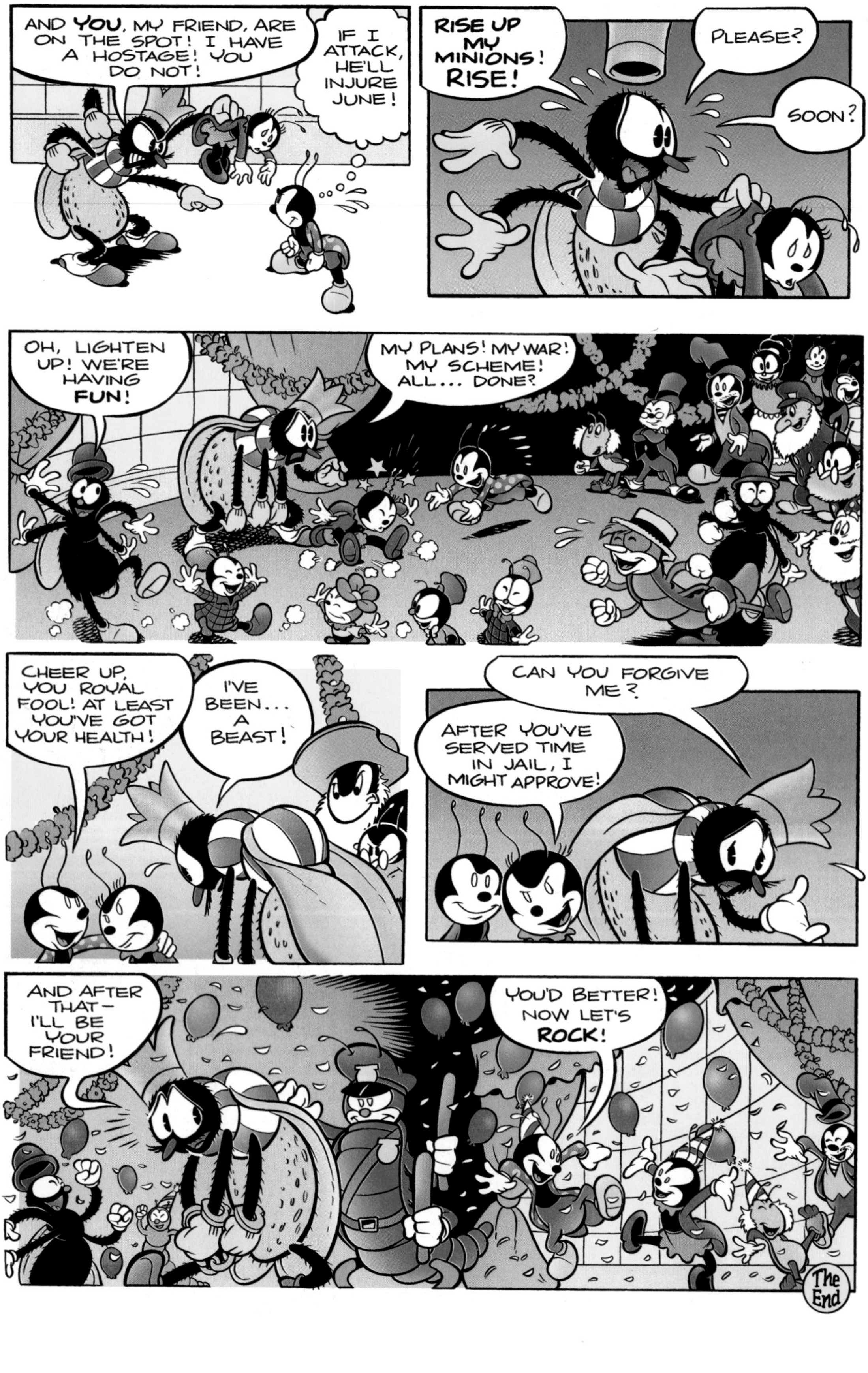
AND YOU, MY FRIEND, ARE ON THE SPOT! I HAVE A HOSTAGE! YOU DO NOT!
IF I ATTACK, HE'LL INJURE JUNE!
RISE UP MY MINIONS! RISE!
PLEASE?
SOON?
OH, LIGHTEN UP! WE'RE HAVING FUN!
MY PLANS! MY WAR! MY SCHEME! ALL... DONE?
CHEER UP, YOU ROYAL FOOL! AT LEAST YOU'VE GOT YOUR HEALTH!
I'VE BEEN... A BEAST!
CAN YOU FORGIVE ME?
AFTER YOU'VE SERVED TIME IN JAIL, I MIGHT APPROVE!
AND AFTER THAT— I'LL BE YOUR FRIEND!
YOU'D BETTER! NOW LET'S ROCK!
The End

BUCKY BUG by Walt Disney

in The Old Folks' New Home

ZS 33-04-23

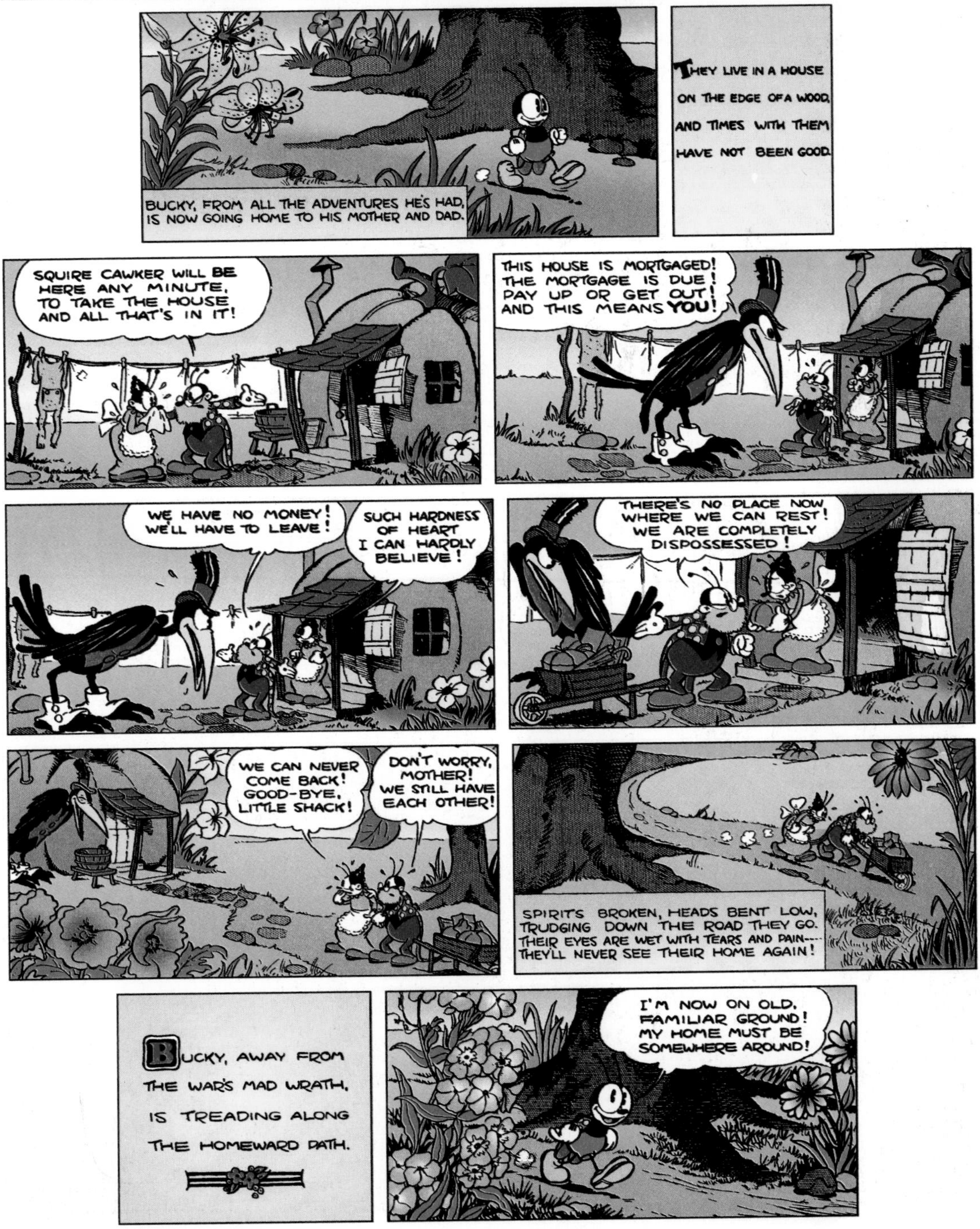

BUCKY, FROM ALL THE ADVENTURES HE'S HAD, IS NOW GOING HOME TO HIS MOTHER AND DAD.
THEY LIVE IN A HOUSE ON THE EDGE OF A WOOD, AND TIMES WITH THEM HAVE NOT BEEN GOOD.
SQUIRE CAWKER WILL BE HERE ANY MINUTE, TO TAKE THE HOUSE AND ALL THAT'S IN IT!
THIS HOUSE IS MORTGAGED! THE MORTGAGE IS DUE! PAY UP OR GET OUT! AND THIS MEANS YOU!
WE HAVE NO MONEY! WE'LL HAVE TO LEAVE!
SUCH HARDNESS OF HEART I CAN HARDLY BELIEVE!
THERE'S NO PLACE NOW WHERE WE CAN REST! WE ARE COMPLETELY DISPOSSESSED!
WE CAN NEVER COME BACK! GOOD-BYE, LITTLE SHACK!
DON'T WORRY, MOTHER! WE STILL HAVE EACH OTHER!
SPIRITS BROKEN, HEADS BENT LOW, TRUDGING DOWN THE ROAD THEY GO. THEIR EYES ARE WET WITH TEARS AND PAIN---- THEY'LL NEVER SEE THEIR HOME AGAIN!
BUCKY, AWAY FROM THE WAR'S MAD WRATH, IS TREADING ALONG THE HOMEWARD PATH.
I'M NOW ON OLD, FAMILIAR GROUND! MY HOME MUST BE SOMEWHERE AROUND!

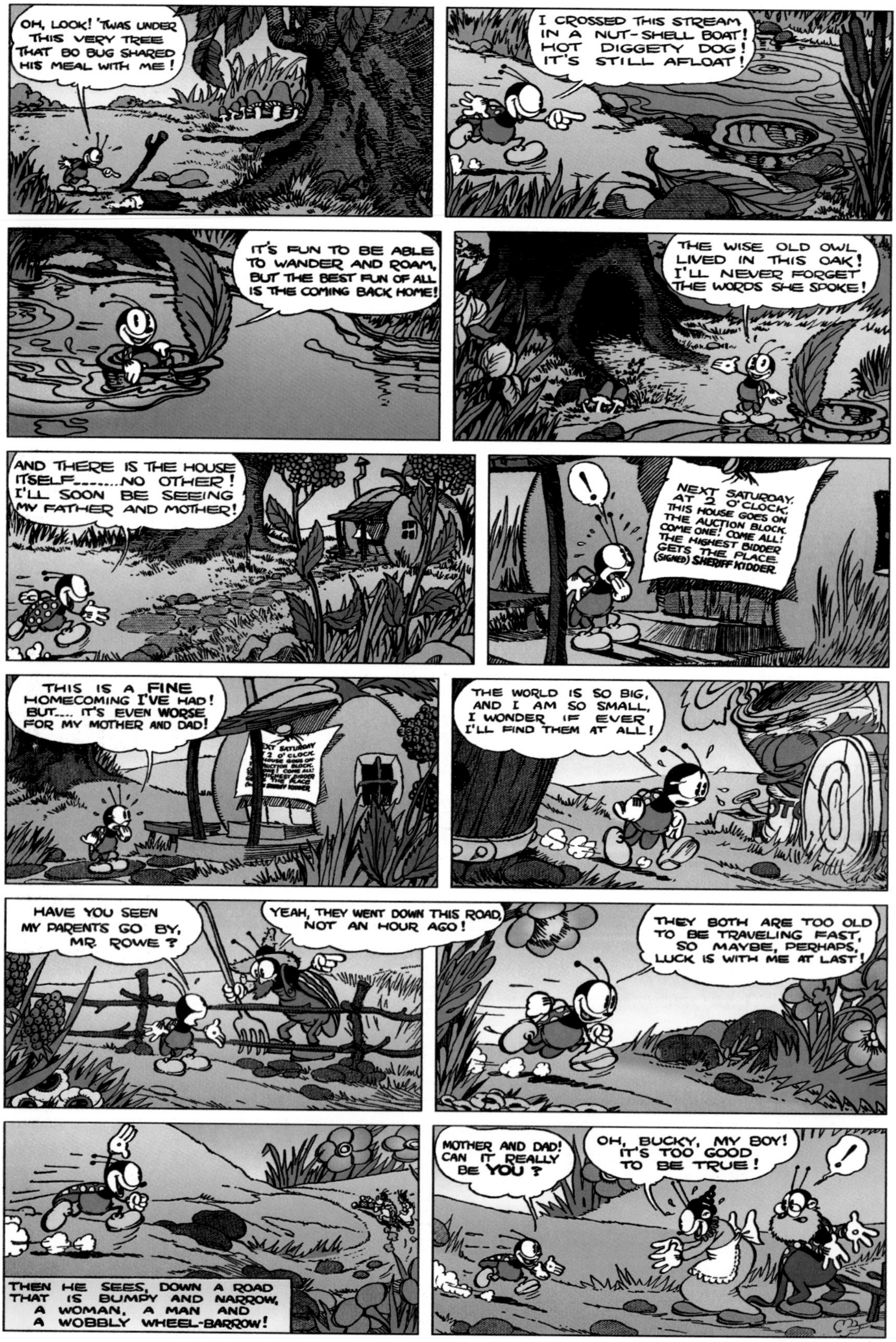
OH, LOOK! 'TWAS UNDER THIS VERY TREE THAT BO BUG SHARED HIS MEAL WITH ME!
I CROSSED THIS STREAM IN A NUT-SHELL BOAT! HOT DIGGETY DOG! IT'S STILL AFLOAT!
IT'S FUN TO BE ABLE TO WANDER AND ROAM, BUT THE BEST FUN OF ALL IS THE COMING BACK HOME!
THE WISE OLD OWL LIVED IN THIS OAK! I'LL NEVER FORGET THE WORDS SHE SPOKE!
AND THERE IS THE HOUSE ITSELF........NO OTHER! I'LL SOON BE SEEING MY FATHER AND MOTHER!
!
NEXT SATURDAY, AT 2 O'CLOCK, THIS HOUSE GOES ON THE AUCTION BLOCK. COME ONE! COME ALL! THE HIGHEST BIDDER GETS THE PLACE. (SIGNED) SHERIFF KIDDER.
THIS IS A FINE HOMECOMING I'VE HAD! BUT.... IT'S EVEN WORSE FOR MY MOTHER AND DAD!
THE WORLD IS SO BIG, AND I AM SO SMALL, I WONDER IF EVER I'LL FIND THEM AT ALL!
HAVE YOU SEEN MY PARENTS GO BY, MR. ROWE?
YEAH, THEY WENT DOWN THIS ROAD, NOT AN HOUR AGO!
THEY BOTH ARE TOO OLD TO BE TRAVELING FAST, SO MAYBE, PERHAPS, LUCK IS WITH ME AT LAST!
THEN HE SEES, DOWN A ROAD THAT IS BUMPY AND NARROW, A WOMAN, A MAN AND A WOBBLY WHEEL-BARROW!
MOTHER AND DAD! CAN IT REALLY BE YOU?
OH, BUCKY, MY BOY! IT'S TOO GOOD TO BE TRUE!
!

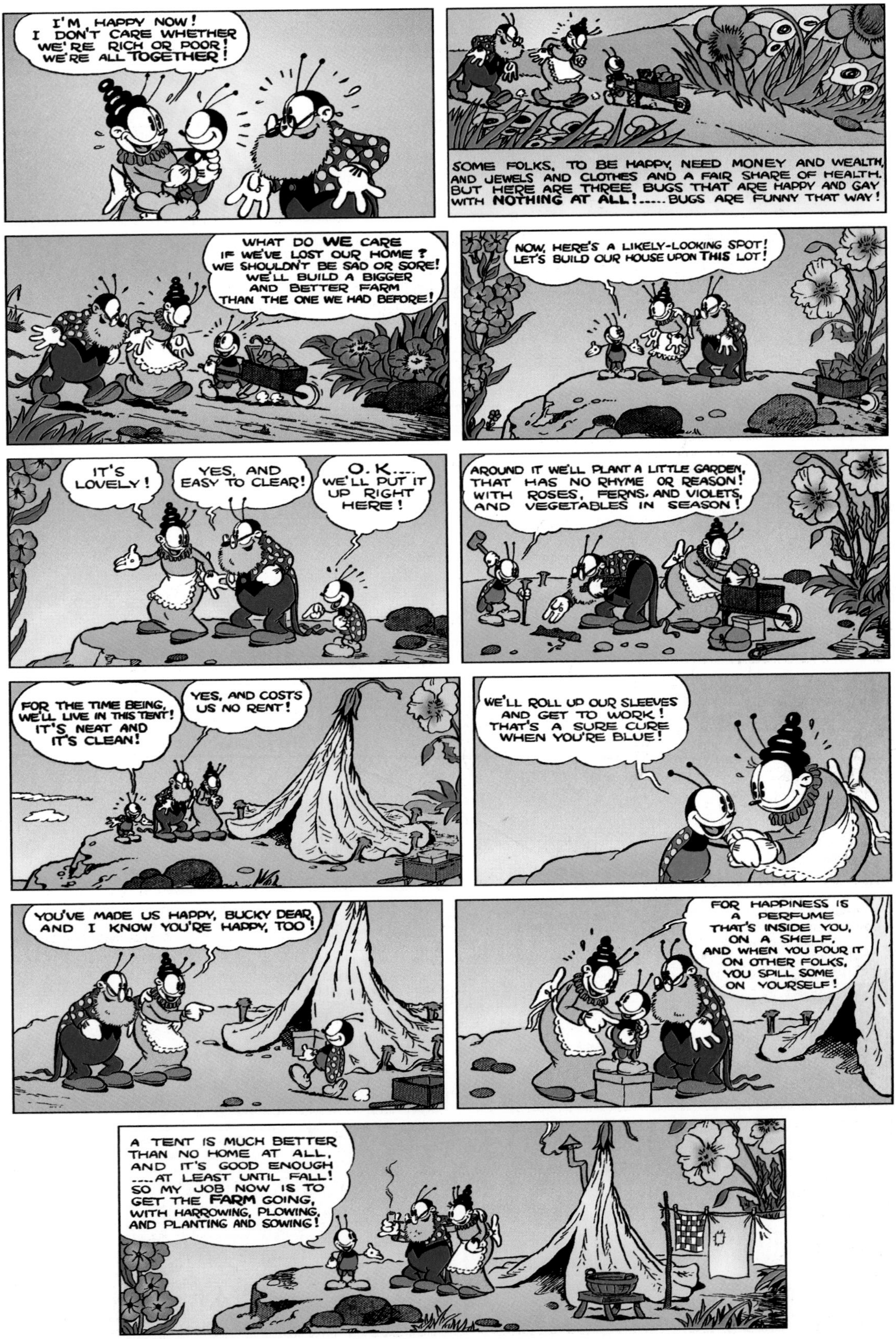
I'M HAPPY NOW! I DON'T CARE WHETHER WE'RE RICH OR POOR! WE'RE ALL TOGETHER!
SOME FOLKS, TO BE HAPPY, NEED MONEY AND WEALTH, AND JEWELS AND CLOTHES AND A FAIR SHARE OF HEALTH. BUT HERE ARE THREE BUGS THAT ARE HAPPY AND GAY WITH NOTHING AT ALL!..... BUGS ARE FUNNY THAT WAY!
WHAT DO WE CARE IF WE'VE LOST OUR HOME? WE SHOULDN'T BE SAD OR SORE! WE'LL BUILD A BIGGER AND BETTER FARM THAN THE ONE WE HAD BEFORE!
NOW, HERE'S A LIKELY-LOOKING SPOT! LET'S BUILD OUR HOUSE UPON THIS LOT!
IT'S LOVELY!
YES, AND EASY TO CLEAR!
O.K.... WE'LL PUT IT UP RIGHT HERE!
AROUND IT WE'LL PLANT A LITTLE GARDEN, THAT HAS NO RHYME OR REASON! WITH ROSES, FERNS, AND VIOLETS, AND VEGETABLES IN SEASON!
FOR THE TIME BEING, WE'LL LIVE IN THIS TENT! IT'S NEAT AND IT'S CLEAN!
YES, AND COSTS US NO RENT!
WE'LL ROLL UP OUR SLEEVES AND GET TO WORK! THAT'S A SURE CURE WHEN YOU'RE BLUE!
YOU'VE MADE US HAPPY, BUCKY DEAR, AND I KNOW YOU'RE HAPPY, TOO!
FOR HAPPINESS IS A PERFUME THAT'S INSIDE YOU, ON A SHELF, AND WHEN YOU POUR IT ON OTHER FOLKS, YOU SPILL SOME ON YOURSELF!
A TENT IS MUCH BETTER THAN NO HOME AT ALL, AND IT'S GOOD ENOUGH ....AT LEAST UNTIL FALL! SO MY JOB NOW IS TO GET THE FARM GOING, WITH HARROWING, PLOWING, AND PLANTING AND SOWING!

WITH BUCKY, IT'S NO SOONER SAID THAN DONE, AND, LOOK! HIS SPRING PLOWING'S ALREADY BEGUN!

A SECOND-HAND RAZOR SOMEONE THREW AWAY IS USED FOR A HARROW THE REST OF THE DAY.

HI-LO, HI-LOO, HI-LAY, HI-LEE! A FARMER'S LIFE IS THE LIFE FOR ME!

A WEE BIT OF SMOOTHING IS ALL THE GROUND NEEDS, TO BE READY FOR PLANTING A FEW MILLION SEEDS!

FOR SOWING THE SEEDS I'VE GOT A SWELL PLAN! I'LL PUT THEM ALL IN THIS TALCUM CAN!

SEEDS

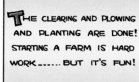

A FARMER'S SONG IS A HAPPY SONG, HI-LEE, HI-LAY, HI-LOW! I DO MY BEST, AND THE GROUND DOES THE REST, HI-LEEDY,- HI-LADY, HI-LOW!

SOWING A SEED IS LIKE A GOOD DEED; YOU DO IT......... AND THEN YOU'RE IN CLOVER! FOR BOTH TAKE ROOT, AND UP THEY SHOOT, AND COME BACK TO YOU, MANY TIMES OVER!

THE CLEARING AND PLOWING AND PLANTING ARE DONE! STARTING A FARM IS HARD WORK...... BUT IT'S FUN!

THE NEXT BIG JOB FOR ME, I GUESS, IS FINDING A PERMANENT HOUSE... NO LESS!

OHHHHHHHHH THE MEADOW-LARK IS ON A LARK, THE HUMMING BIRD IS HUMMING, THE ROBINS ROB, THE BUZZARDS BUZZ, AND THE BUMBLE BEE IS BUMMING!

LOOK AT THE PUMPKINS! WHOOPS, MY DEAR! I KNOW I'LL BE ABLE TO FIND ONE HERE!

THIS IS A BEAUTY! IT'S BIG AND IT'S PLAIN! BUT.....GETTING IT HOME'S SOMETHING ELSE AGAIN!

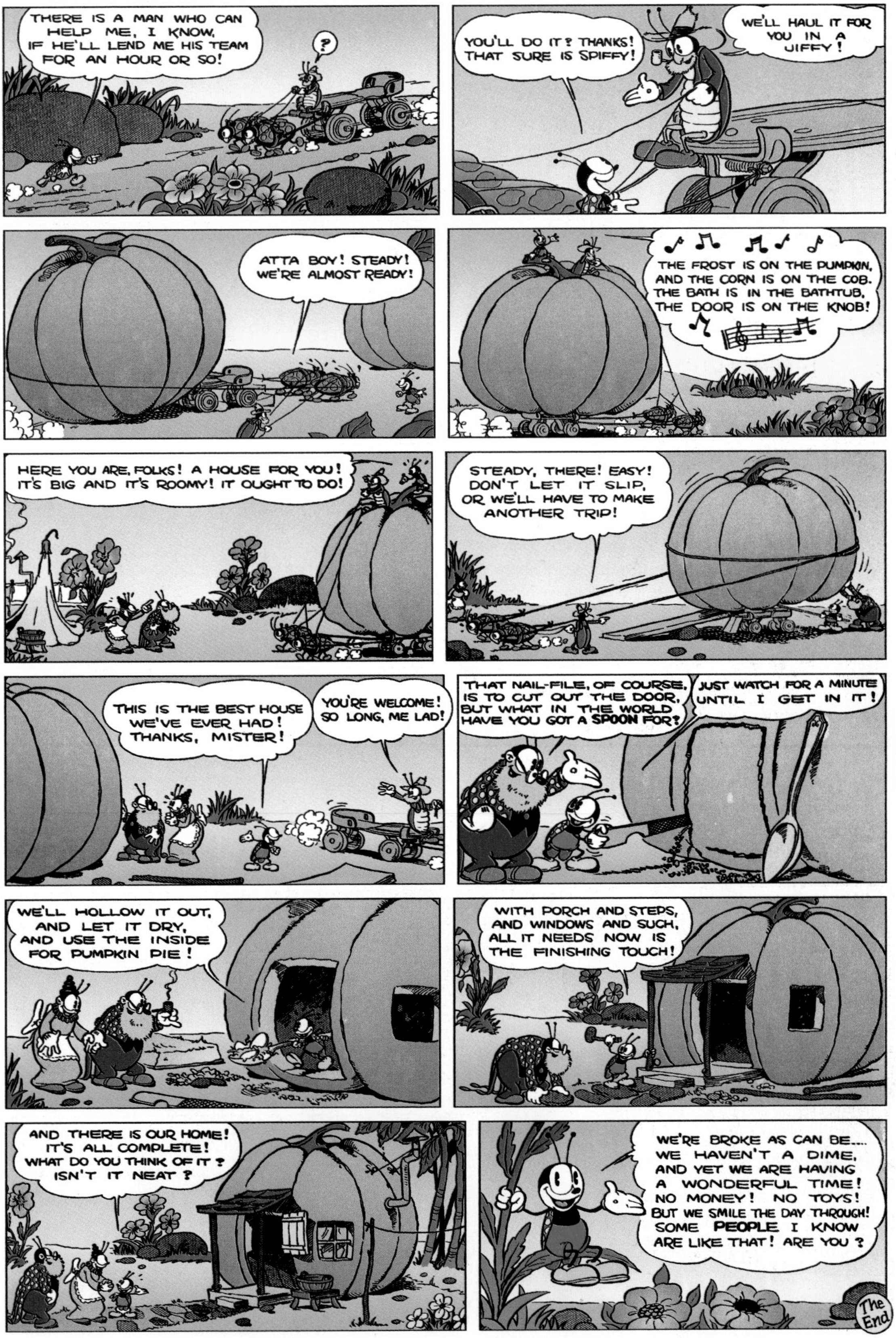
THERE IS A MAN WHO CAN HELP ME, I KNOW, IF HE'LL LEND ME HIS TEAM FOR AN HOUR OR SO!
?
YOU'LL DO IT? THANKS! THAT SURE IS SPIFFY!
WE'LL HAUL IT FOR YOU IN A JIFFY!
ATTA BOY! STEADY! WE'RE ALMOST READY!
THE FROST IS ON THE PUMPKIN, AND THE CORN IS ON THE COB. THE BATH IS IN THE BATHTUB, THE DOOR IS ON THE KNOB!
HERE YOU ARE, FOLKS! A HOUSE FOR YOU! IT'S BIG AND IT'S ROOMY! IT OUGHT TO DO!
STEADY, THERE! EASY! DON'T LET IT SLIP, OR WE'LL HAVE TO MAKE ANOTHER TRIP!
THIS IS THE BEST HOUSE WE'VE EVER HAD! THANKS, MISTER!
YOU'RE WELCOME! SO LONG, ME LAD!
THAT NAIL-FILE, OF COURSE, IS TO CUT OUT THE DOOR, BUT WHAT IN THE WORLD HAVE YOU GOT A SPOON FOR?
JUST WATCH FOR A MINUTE UNTIL I GET IN IT!
WE'LL HOLLOW IT OUT, AND LET IT DRY, AND USE THE INSIDE FOR PUMPKIN PIE!
WITH PORCH AND STEPS, AND WINDOWS AND SUCH, ALL IT NEEDS NOW IS THE FINISHING TOUCH!
AND THERE IS OUR HOME! IT'S ALL COMPLETE! WHAT DO YOU THINK OF IT? ISN'T IT NEAT?
WE'RE BROKE AS CAN BE.... WE HAVEN'T A DIME, AND YET WE ARE HAVING A WONDERFUL TIME! NO MONEY! NO TOYS! BUT WE SMILE THE DAY THROUGH! SOME PEOPLE I KNOW ARE LIKE THAT! ARE YOU?
The End

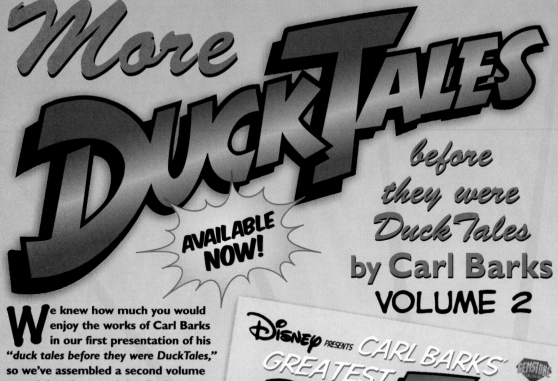

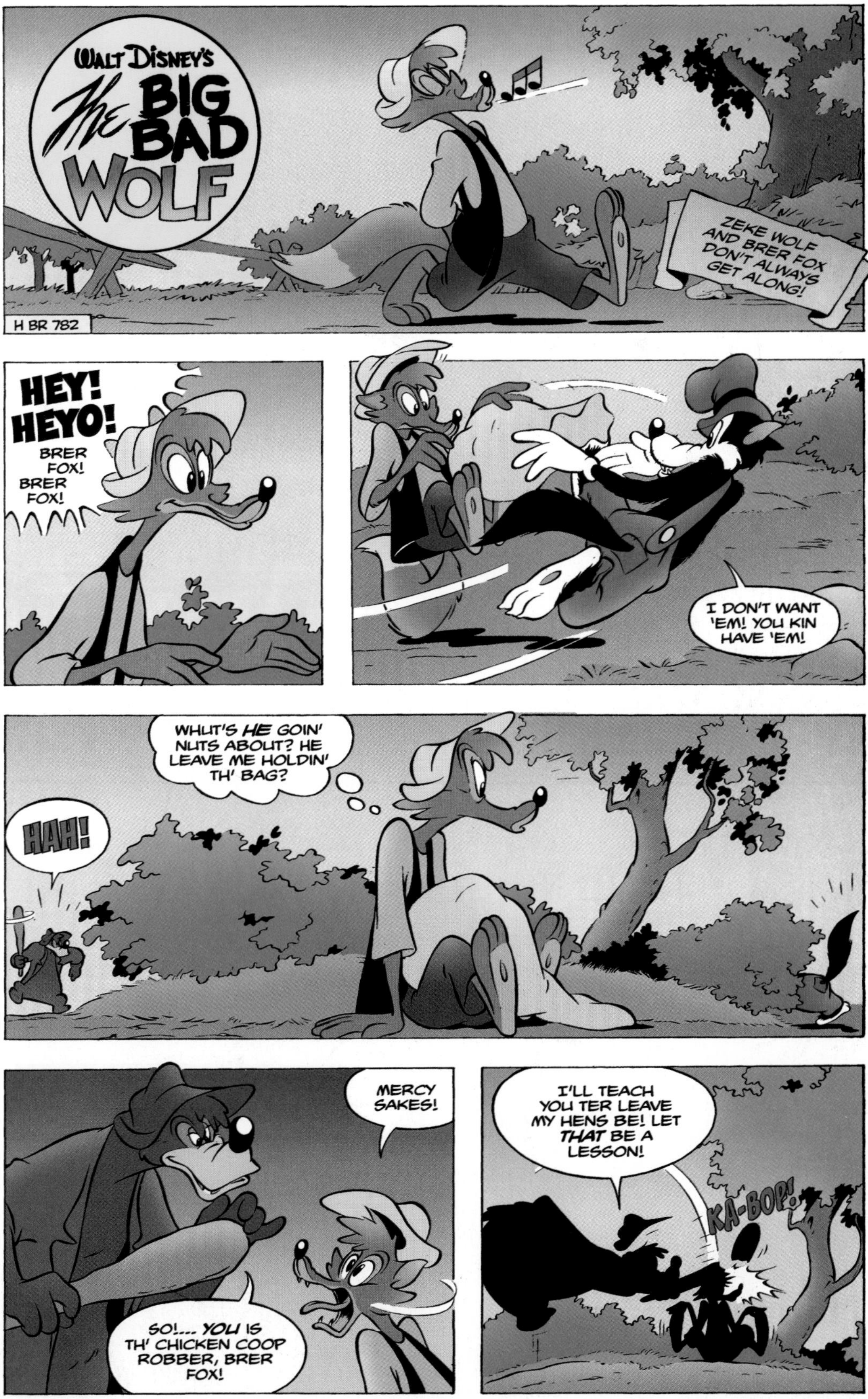
WALT DISNEY'S THE BIG BAD WOLF
ZEKE WOLF AND BRER FOX DON'T ALWAYS GET ALONG!
H BR 782
HEY! HEYO!
BRER FOX! BRER FOX!
I DON'T WANT 'EM! YOU KIN HAVE 'EM!
WHUT'S HE GOIN' NUTS ABOUT? HE LEAVE ME HOLDIN' TH' BAG?
HAH!
MERCY SAKES!
SO!... YOU IS TH' CHICKEN COOP ROBBER, BRER FOX!
I'LL TEACH YOU TER LEAVE MY HENS BE! LET THAT BE A LESSON!
KA-BOP!

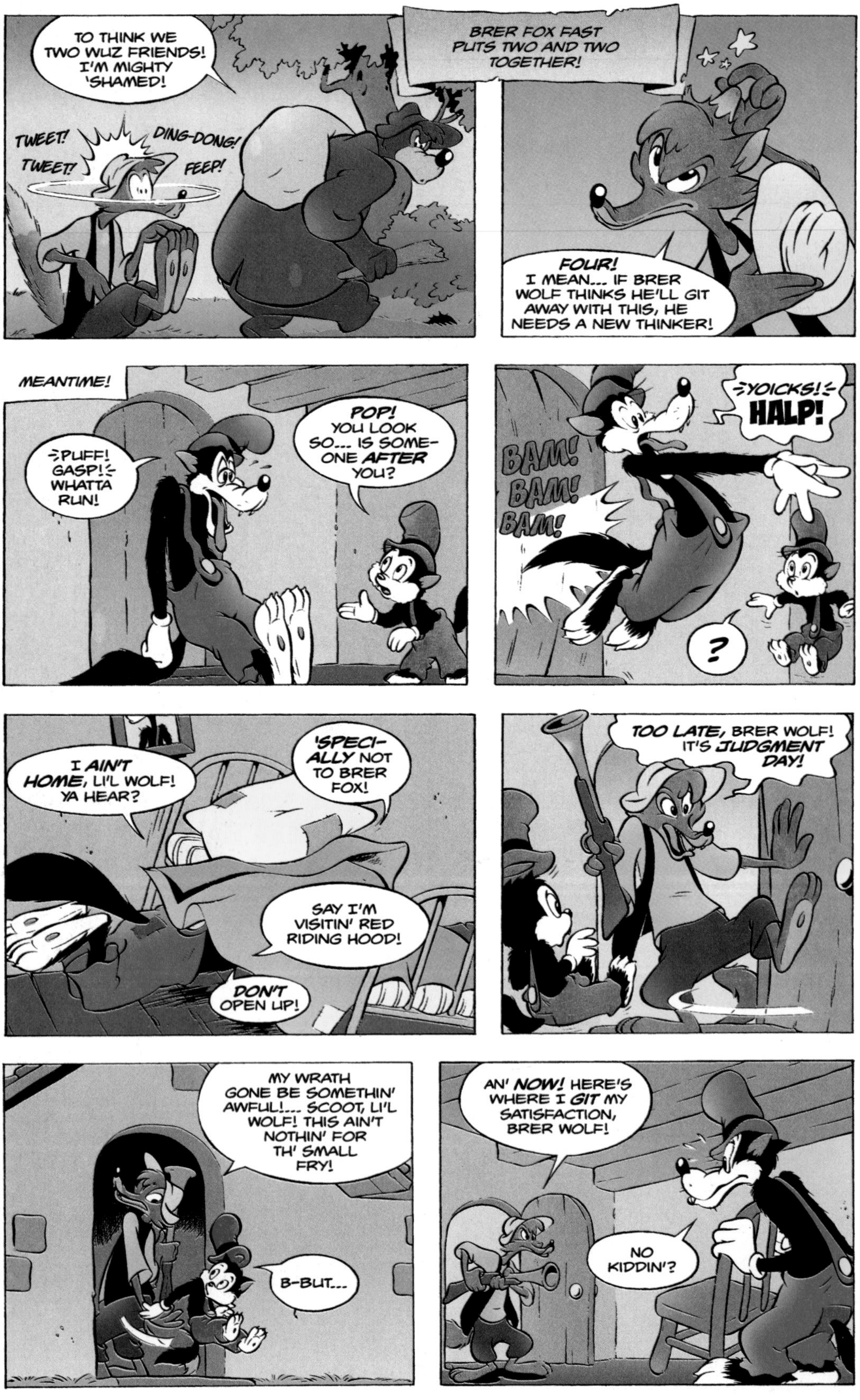

TO THINK WE TWO WUZ FRIENDS! I'M MIGHTY 'SHAMED!
TWEET! TWEET!
DING-DONG!
FEEP!
BRER FOX FAST PUTS TWO AND TWO TOGETHER!
FOUR! I MEAN... IF BRER WOLF THINKS HE'LL GIT AWAY WITH THIS, HE NEEDS A NEW THINKER!
MEANTIME!
PUFF! GASP! WHATTA RUN!
POP! YOU LOOK SO... IS SOME-ONE AFTER YOU?
BAM! BAM! BAM!
YOICKS! HALP!
?
I AIN'T HOME, LI'L WOLF! YA HEAR?
'SPECI-ALLY NOT TO BRER FOX!
SAY I'M VISITIN' RED RIDING HOOD!
DON'T OPEN UP!
TOO LATE, BRER WOLF! IT'S JUDGMENT DAY!
MY WRATH GONE BE SOMETHIN' AWFUL!... SCOOT, LI'L WOLF! THIS AIN'T NOTHIN' FOR TH' SMALL FRY!
B-BUT...
AN' NOW! HERE'S WHERE I GIT MY SATISFACTION, BRER WOLF!
NO KIDDIN'?

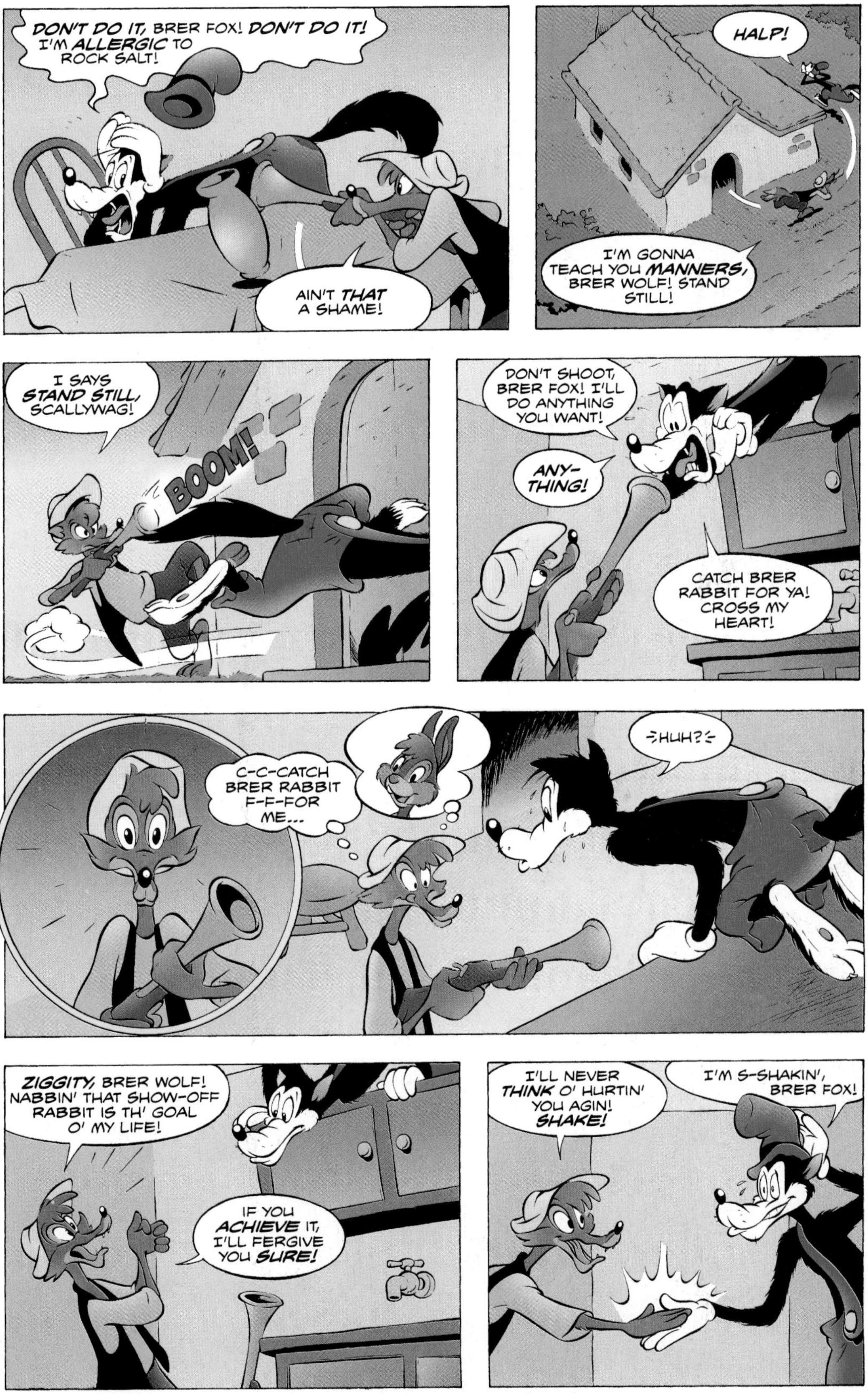

DON'T DO IT, BRER FOX! DON'T DO IT! I'M ALLERGIC TO ROCK SALT!
AIN'T THAT A SHAME!
HALP!
I'M GONNA TEACH YOU MANNERS, BRER WOLF! STAND STILL!
I SAYS STAND STILL, SCALLYWAG!
BOOM!
DON'T SHOOT, BRER FOX! I'LL DO ANYTHING YOU WANT!
ANY-THING!
CATCH BRER RABBIT FOR YA! CROSS MY HEART!
C-C-CATCH BRER RABBIT F-F-FOR ME...
HUH?
ZIGGITY, BRER WOLF! NABBIN' THAT SHOW-OFF RABBIT IS TH' GOAL O' MY LIFE!
IF YOU ACHIEVE IT, I'LL FERGIVE YOU SURE!
I'LL NEVER THINK O' HURTIN' YOU AGIN! SHAKE!
I'M S-SHAKIN', BRER FOX!

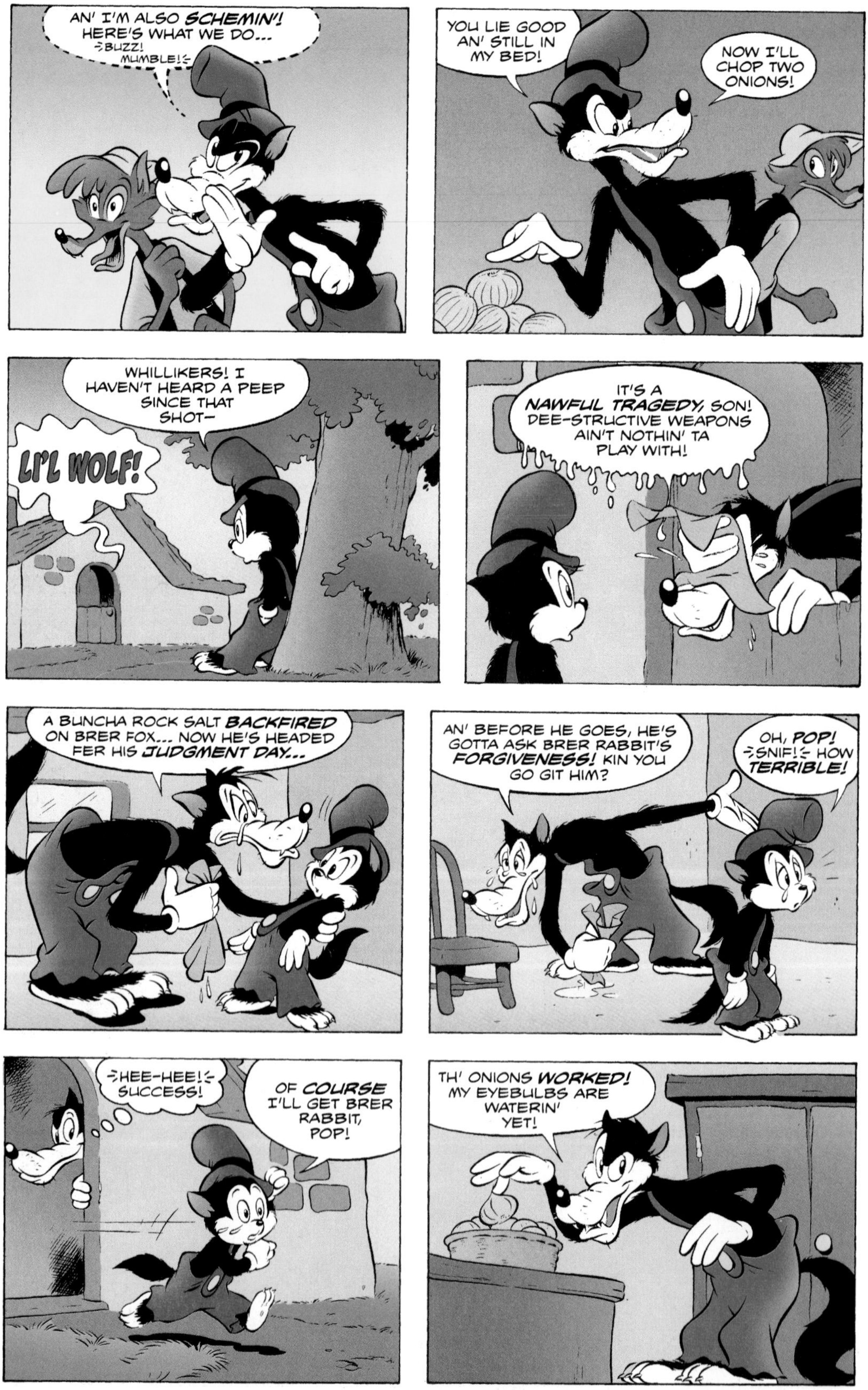
AN' I'M ALSO SCHEMIN'! HERE'S WHAT WE DO... BUZZ! MUMBLE!
YOU LIE GOOD AN' STILL IN MY BED!
NOW I'LL CHOP TWO ONIONS!
WHILLIKERS! I HAVEN'T HEARD A PEEP SINCE THAT SHOT—
LI'L WOLF!
IT'S A NAWFUL TRAGEDY, SON! DEE-STRUCTIVE WEAPONS AIN'T NOTHIN' TA PLAY WITH!
A BUNCHA ROCK SALT BACKFIRED ON BRER FOX... NOW HE'S HEADED FER HIS JUDGMENT DAY...
AN' BEFORE HE GOES, HE'S GOTTA ASK BRER RABBIT'S FORGIVENESS! KIN YOU GO GIT HIM?
OH, POP! SNIF! HOW TERRIBLE!
HEE-HEE! SUCCESS!
OF COURSE I'LL GET BRER RABBIT, POP!
TH' ONIONS WORKED! MY EYEBULBS ARE WATERIN' YET!

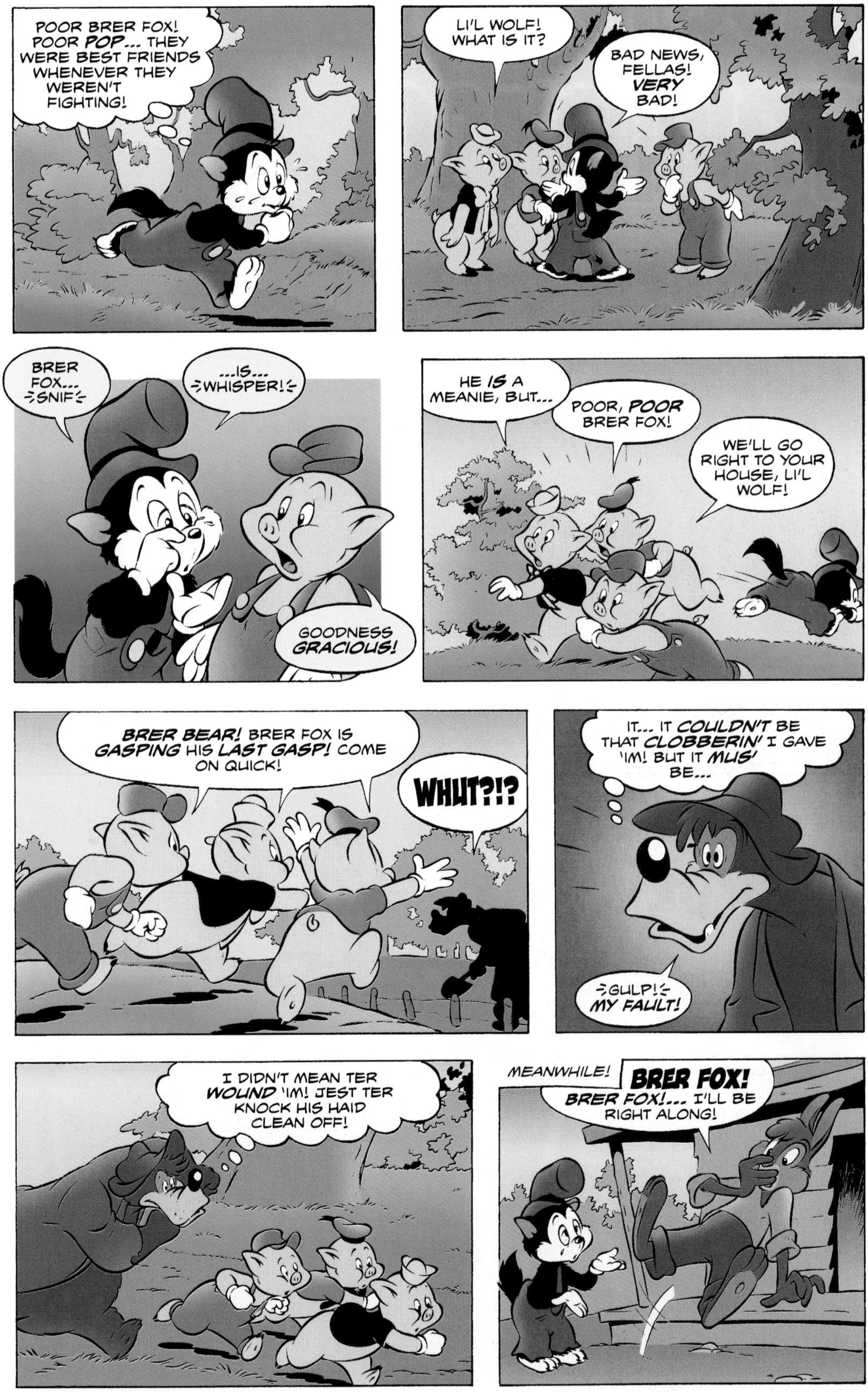
POOR BRER FOX! POOR POP... THEY WERE BEST FRIENDS WHENEVER THEY WEREN'T FIGHTING!
LI'L WOLF! WHAT IS IT?
BAD NEWS, FELLAS! VERY BAD!
BRER FOX... SNIF
...IS... WHISPER!
GOODNESS GRACIOUS!
HE IS A MEANIE, BUT...
POOR, POOR BRER FOX!
WE'LL GO RIGHT TO YOUR HOUSE, LI'L WOLF!
BRER BEAR! BRER FOX IS GASPING HIS LAST GASP! COME ON QUICK!
WHUT?!?
IT... IT COULDN'T BE THAT CLOBBERIN' I GAVE 'IM! BUT IT MUS' BE...
GULP! MY FAULT!
I DIDN'T MEAN TER WOUND 'IM! JEST TER KNOCK HIS HAID CLEAN OFF!
MEANWHILE!
BRER FOX!
BRER FOX!... I'LL BE RIGHT ALONG!

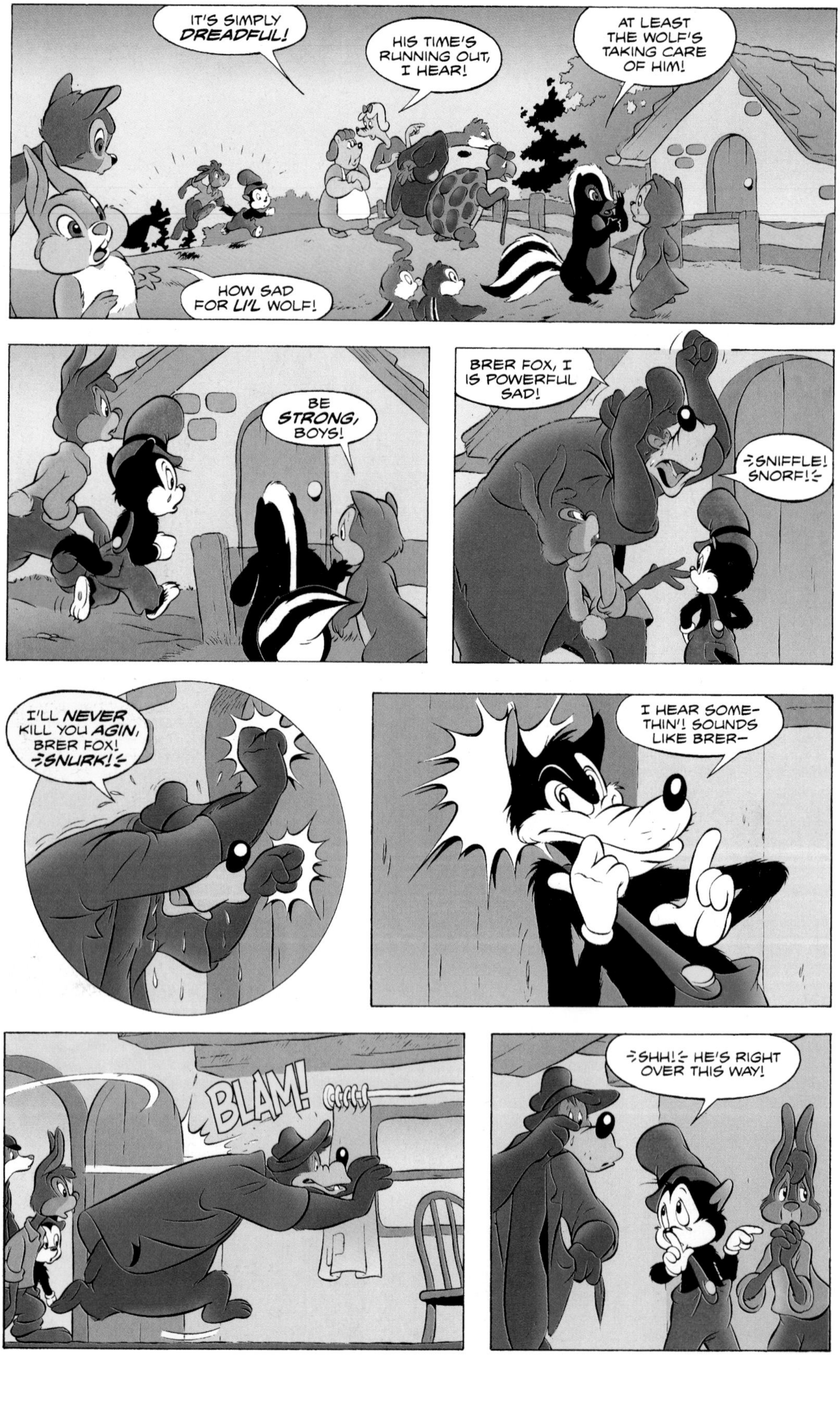
IT'S SIMPLY DREADFUL!
HIS TIME'S RUNNING OUT, I HEAR!
AT LEAST THE WOLF'S TAKING CARE OF HIM!
HOW SAD FOR LI'L WOLF!
BE STRONG, BOYS!
BRER FOX, I IS POWERFUL SAD!
SNIFFLE! SNORF!
I'LL NEVER KILL YOU AGIN, BRER FOX! SNURK!
I HEAR SOME-THIN'! SOUNDS LIKE BRER–
BLAM!
SHH! HE'S RIGHT OVER THIS WAY!

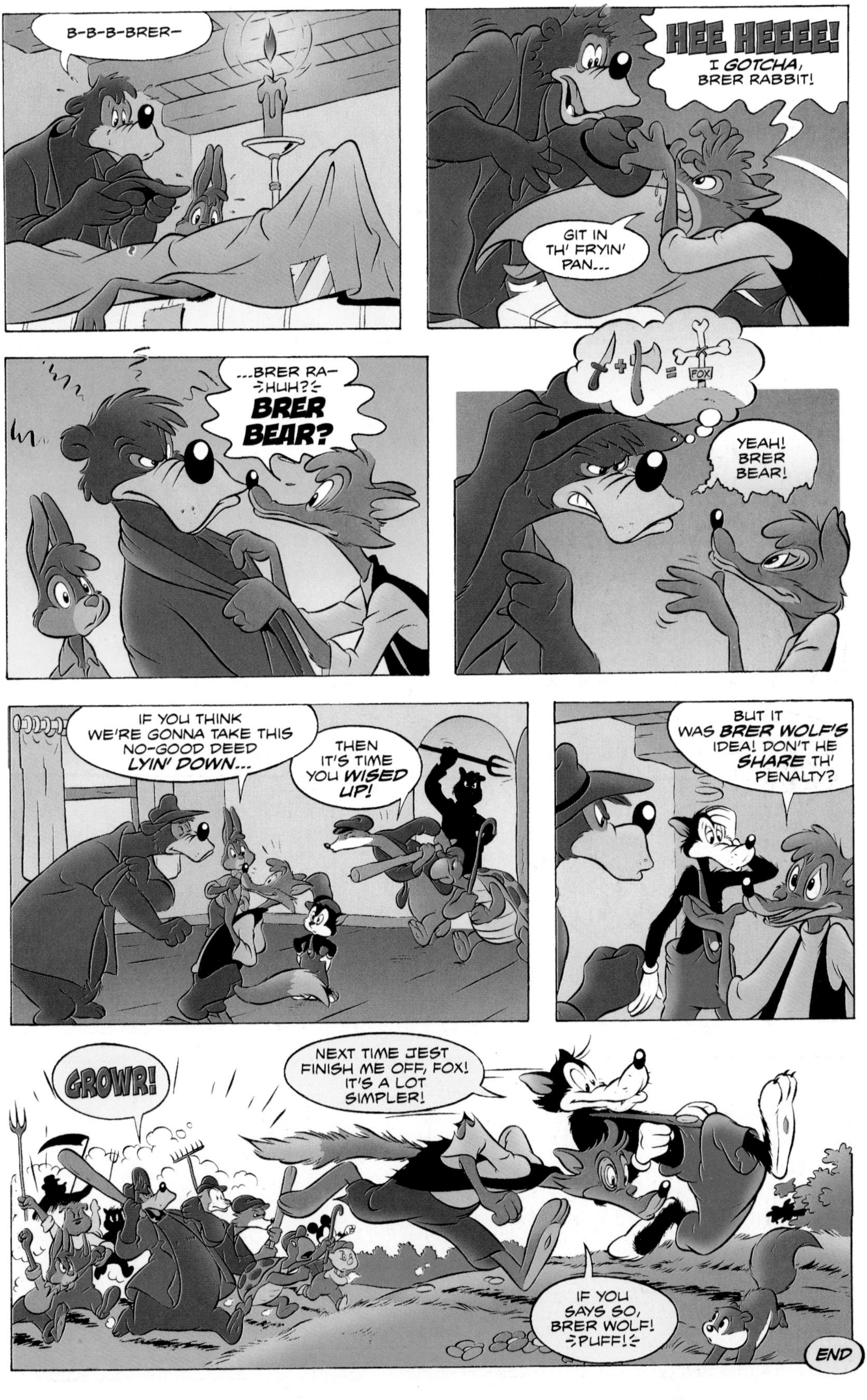
B-B-B-BRER—
HEE HEEEE! I GOTCHA, BRER RABBIT!
GIT IN TH' FRYIN' PAN...
...BRER RA— HUH? BRER BEAR?
FOX
YEAH! BRER BEAR!
IF YOU THINK WE'RE GONNA TAKE THIS NO-GOOD DEED LYIN' DOWN...
THEN IT'S TIME YOU WISED UP!
BUT IT WAS BRER WOLF'S IDEA! DON'T HE SHARE TH' PENALTY?
GROWR!
NEXT TIME JEST FINISH ME OFF, FOX! IT'S A LOT SIMPLER!
IF YOU SAYS SO, BRER WOLF! PUFF!
END

Gemstone Publishing presents

More Life and Times of $crooge McDuck

WALT DISNEY'S
The Life and Times of
$CROOGE McDUCK
Companion
by
DON ROSA

You asked for them, and here they are... the prequels, the sequels, and the in-betweenquels to Don Rosa's *Life and Times of Scrooge McDuck!* Filling in the gaps between the twelve original chapters are "The Cowboy Captain of the Cutty Sark" (Chapter 3B/*Uncle Scrooge* 318), "The Vigilante of Pizen Bluff" (Chapter 6B/*US* 306), "The Prisoner of White Agony Creek" (the all-new Chapter 8B!), "Hearts of the Yukon" (Chapter 8C/*Walt Disney Giant* 1) and "The Sharpie of the Culebra Cut" (Chapter 10B/*US* 332).

But wait... there's more! We've got Don's first look at Scrooge's youth—the famous flashback from "Last Sled to Dawson" (*Uncle Scrooge Adventures* 5). We've got the apocrypha: "Of Ducks and Dimes and Destinies" (Chapter 0/*US* 297) and "The Dream of a Lifetime!" (*US* 329), with the modern-day Magica De Spell and Beagle Boys wreaking havoc in Scrooge's past. And we've got the commentary—more than a dozen pages of Rosa recollections on how these classics came to be, all for only $16.99!

STILL ON SALE (AT A TIGHTWAD-FRIENDLY PRICE!)

It's Rosa's original twelve-chapter quest into Scrooge's life—presented in a 264-page volume replete with extensive authorial commentary. From Scrooge's Scottish childhood to his worldwide quest for gold; from his ill-starred romances to his meetings with history's heroes, this classic biography marked a milestone in duck comics. Annotated by Rosa himself and full of new-to-North-America art, Gemstone's $16.99 collected edition belongs on every Disney fan's bookshelf.

GEMSTONE PUBLISHING

WALT DISNEY'S
The Life and Times of
$CROOGE McDUCK
DON ROSA

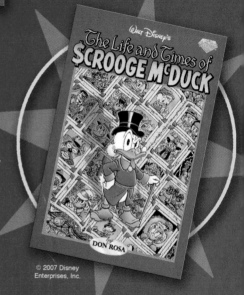

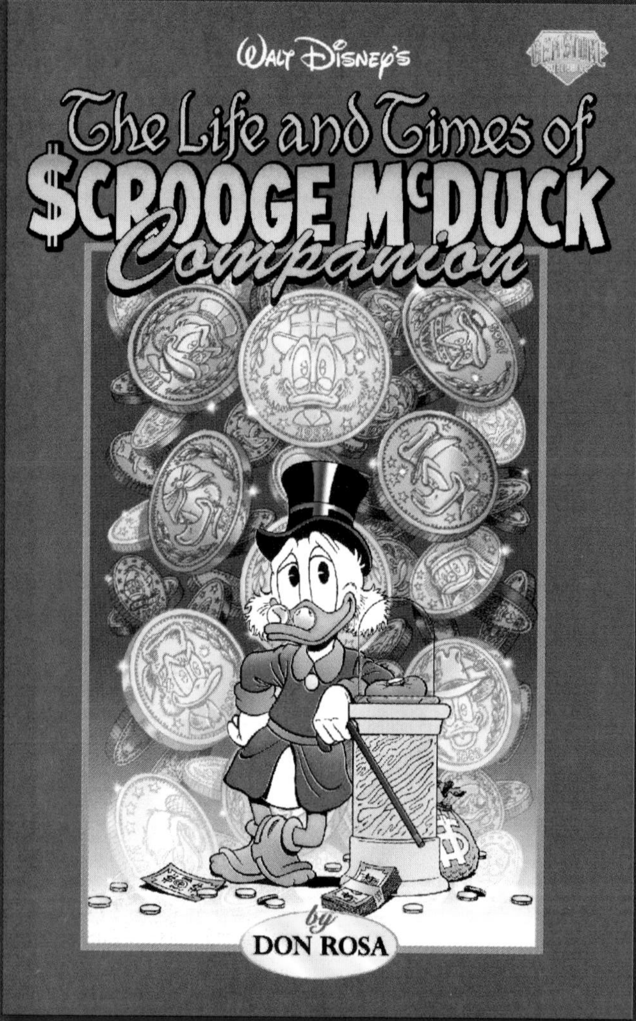

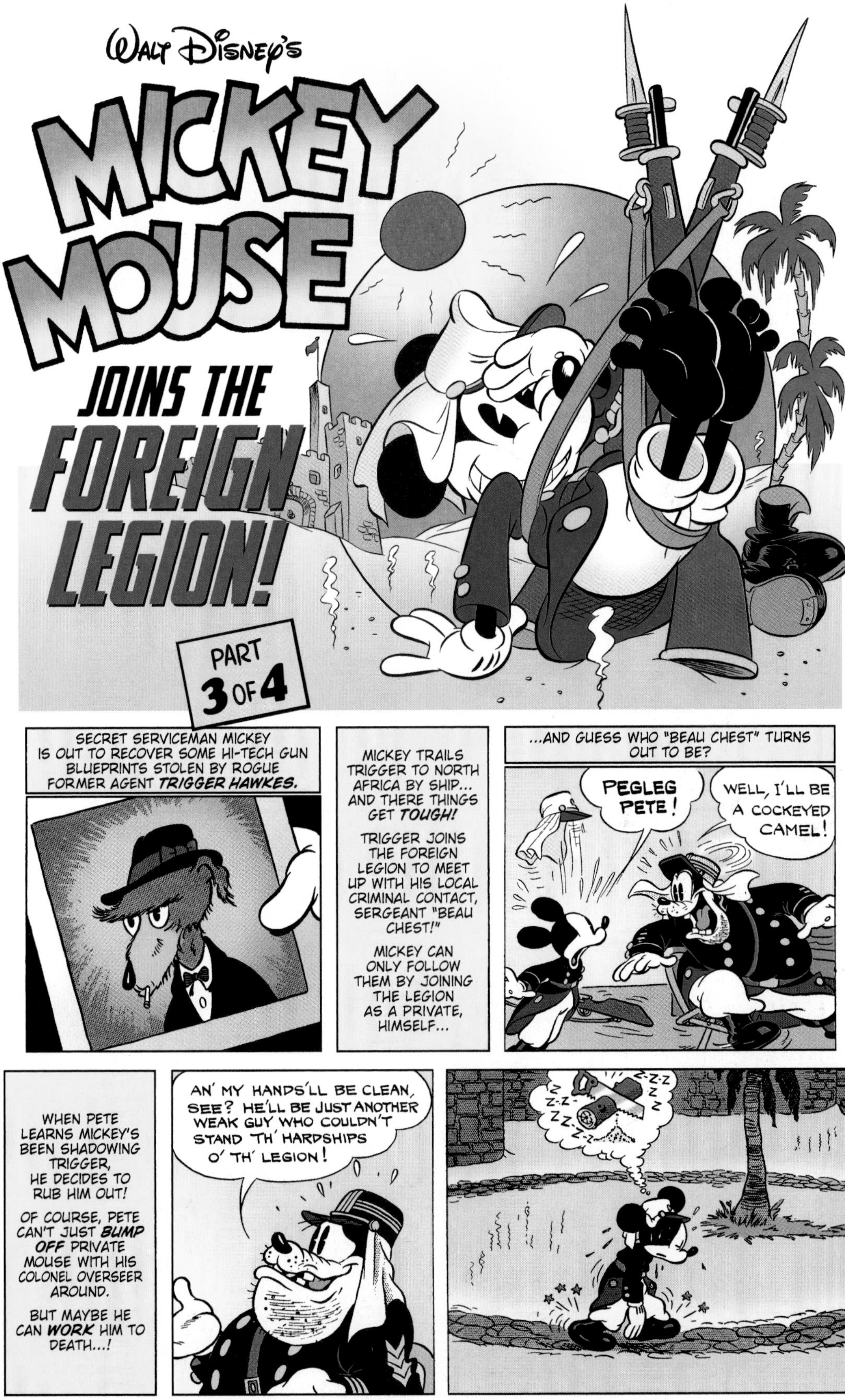
WALT DISNEY'S
MICKEY MOUSE
JOINS THE FOREIGN LEGION!
PART 3 OF 4
SECRET SERVICEMAN MICKEY IS OUT TO RECOVER SOME HI-TECH GUN BLUEPRINTS STOLEN BY ROGUE FORMER AGENT TRIGGER HAWKES.
MICKEY TRAILS TRIGGER TO NORTH AFRICA BY SHIP... AND THERE THINGS GET TOUGH!
TRIGGER JOINS THE FOREIGN LEGION TO MEET UP WITH HIS LOCAL CRIMINAL CONTACT, SERGEANT "BEAU CHEST!"
MICKEY CAN ONLY FOLLOW THEM BY JOINING THE LEGION AS A PRIVATE, HIMSELF...
...AND GUESS WHO "BEAU CHEST" TURNS OUT TO BE?
PEGLEG PETE!
WELL, I'LL BE A COCKEYED CAMEL!
WHEN PETE LEARNS MICKEY'S BEEN SHADOWING TRIGGER, HE DECIDES TO RUB HIM OUT!
OF COURSE, PETE CAN'T JUST BUMP OFF PRIVATE MOUSE WITH HIS COLONEL OVERSEER AROUND.
BUT MAYBE HE CAN WORK HIM TO DEATH...!
AN' MY HANDS'LL BE CLEAN, SEE? HE'LL BE JUST ANOTHER WEAK GUY WHO COULDN'T STAND TH' HARDSHIPS O' TH' LEGION!

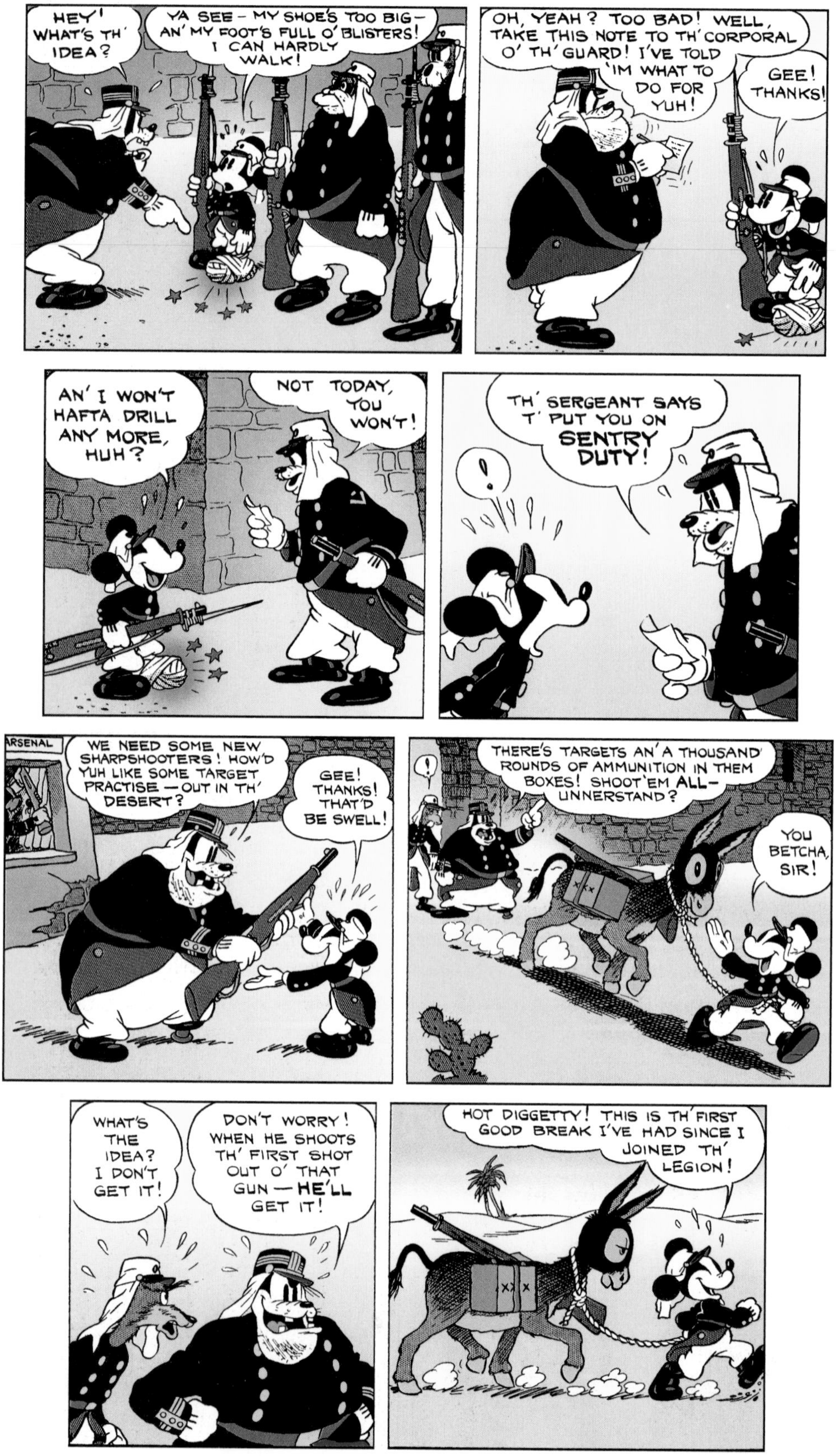
HEY! WHAT'S TH' IDEA?
YA SEE – MY SHOE'S TOO BIG – AN' MY FOOT'S FULL O' BLISTERS! I CAN HARDLY WALK!
OH, YEAH? TOO BAD! WELL, TAKE THIS NOTE TO TH' CORPORAL O' TH' GUARD! I'VE TOLD 'IM WHAT TO DO FOR YUH!
GEE! THANKS!
AN' I WON'T HAFTA DRILL ANY MORE, HUH?
NOT TODAY, YOU WON'T!
TH' SERGEANT SAYS T' PUT YOU ON SENTRY DUTY!
!
ARSENAL
WE NEED SOME NEW SHARPSHOOTERS! HOW'D YUH LIKE SOME TARGET PRACTISE — OUT IN TH' DESERT?
GEE! THANKS! THAT'D BE SWELL!
!
THERE'S TARGETS AN' A THOUSAND ROUNDS OF AMMUNITION IN THEM BOXES! SHOOT 'EM ALL – UNNERSTAND?
YOU BETCHA, SIR!
WHAT'S THE IDEA? I DON'T GET IT!
DON'T WORRY! WHEN HE SHOOTS TH' FIRST SHOT OUT O' THAT GUN — HE'LL GET IT!
HOT DIGGETTY! THIS IS TH' FIRST GOOD BREAK I'VE HAD SINCE I JOINED TH' LEGION!

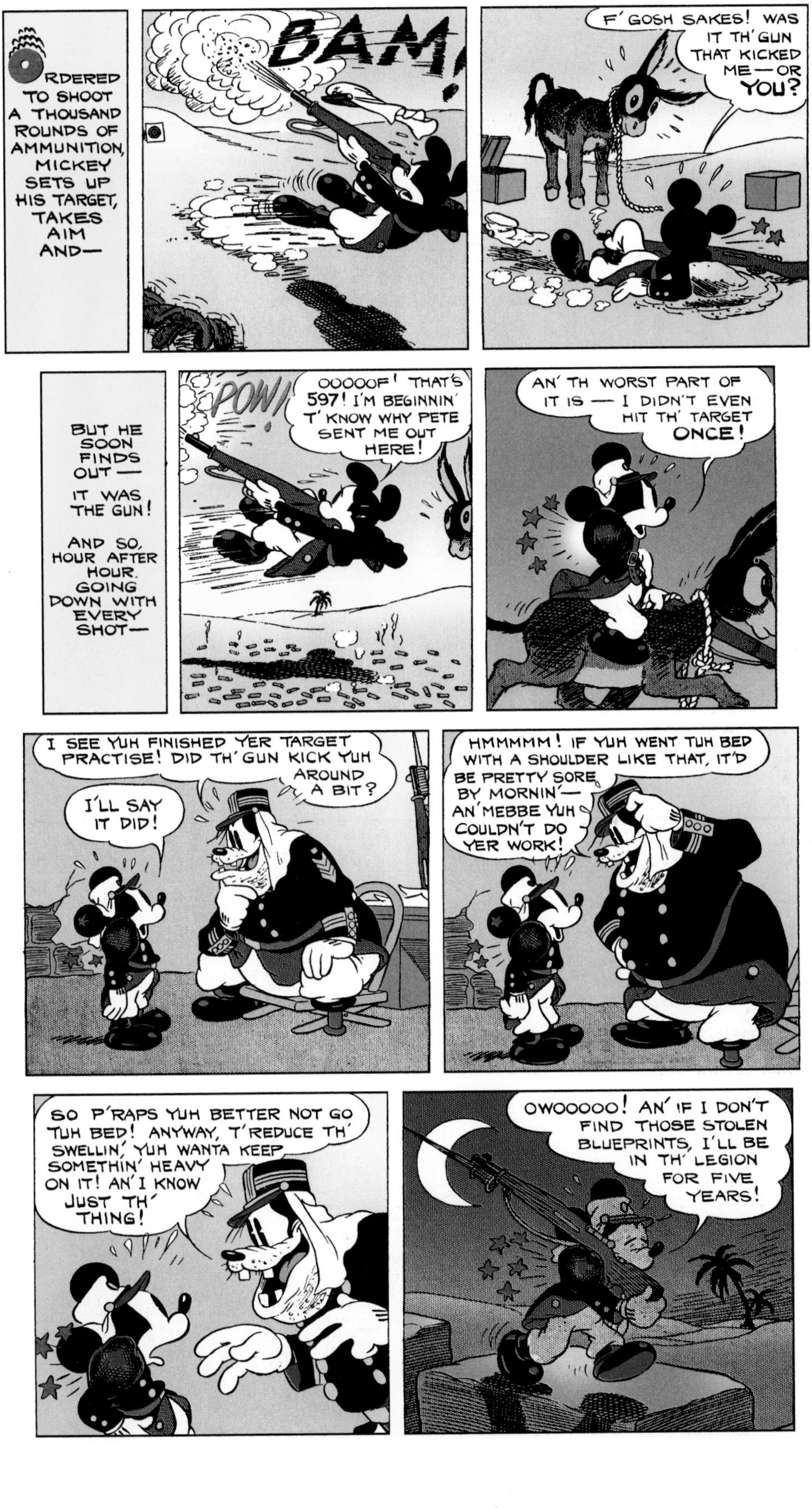
ORDERED TO SHOOT A THOUSAND ROUNDS OF AMMUNITION, MICKEY SETS UP HIS TARGET, TAKES AIM AND—
BAM!
F' GOSH SAKES! WAS IT TH' GUN THAT KICKED ME—OR YOU?
BUT HE SOON FINDS OUT— IT WAS THE GUN!
AND SO, HOUR AFTER HOUR, GOING DOWN WITH EVERY SHOT—
POW!
OOOOOF! THAT'S 597! I'M BEGINNIN' T' KNOW WHY PETE SENT ME OUT HERE!
AN' TH WORST PART OF IT IS — I DIDN'T EVEN HIT TH' TARGET ONCE!
I SEE YUH FINISHED YER TARGET PRACTISE! DID TH' GUN KICK YUH AROUND A BIT?
I'LL SAY IT DID!
HMMMMM! IF YUH WENT TUH BED WITH A SHOULDER LIKE THAT, IT'D BE PRETTY SORE BY MORNIN'— AN' MEBBE YUH COULDN'T DO YER WORK!
SO P'RAPS YUH BETTER NOT GO TUH BED! ANYWAY, T'REDUCE TH' SWELLIN' YUH WANTA KEEP SOMETHIN' HEAVY ON IT! AN' I KNOW JUST TH' THING!
OWOOOOO! AN' IF I DON'T FIND THOSE STOLEN BLUEPRINTS, I'LL BE IN TH' LEGION FOR FIVE YEARS!

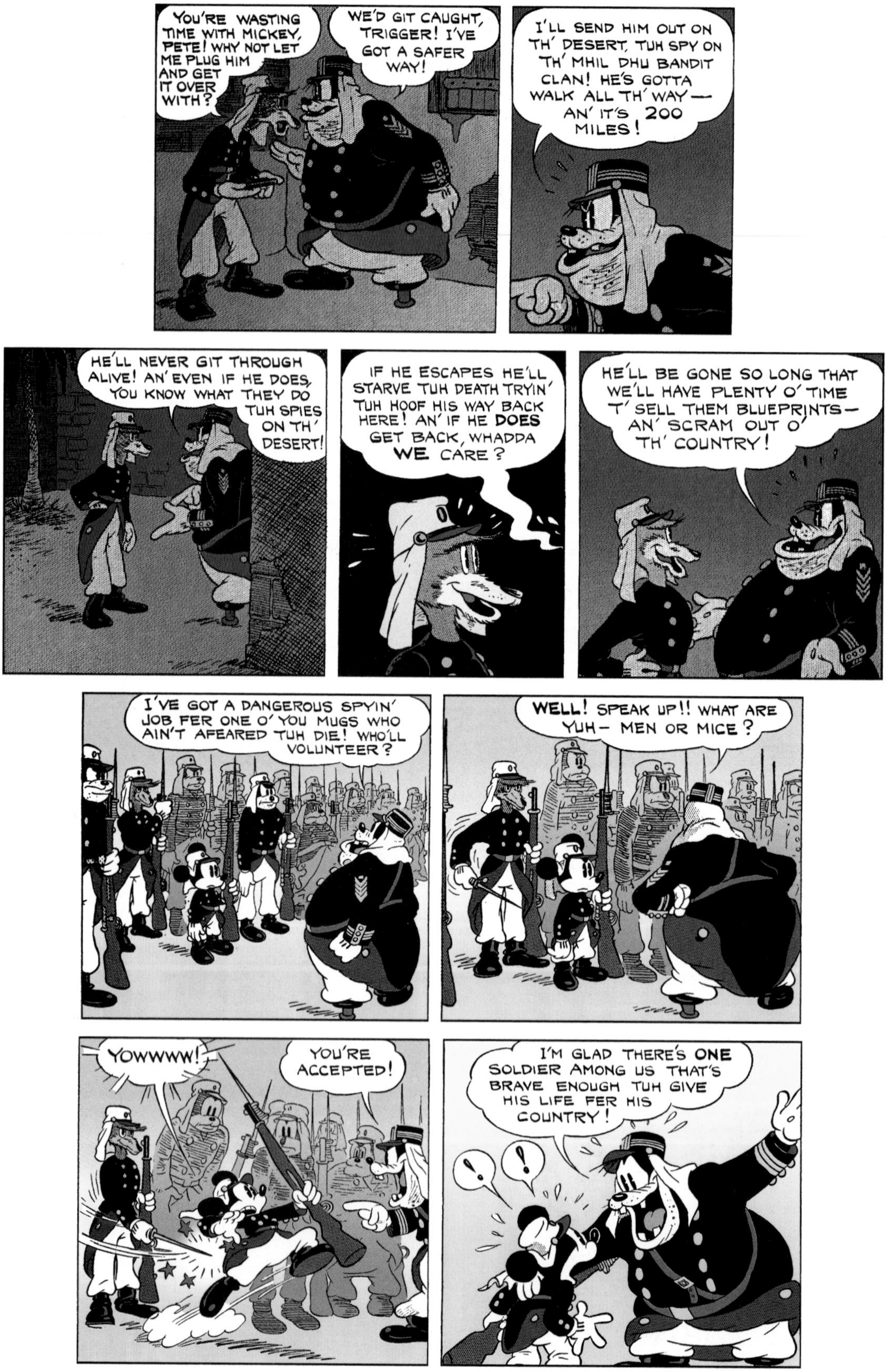
YOU'RE WASTING TIME WITH MICKEY, PETE! WHY NOT LET ME PLUG HIM AND GET IT OVER WITH?
WE'D GIT CAUGHT, TRIGGER! I'VE GOT A SAFER WAY!
I'LL SEND HIM OUT ON TH' DESERT, TUH SPY ON TH' MHIL DHU BANDIT CLAN! HE'S GOTTA WALK ALL TH' WAY— AN' IT'S 200 MILES!
HE'LL NEVER GIT THROUGH ALIVE! AN' EVEN IF HE DOES, YOU KNOW WHAT THEY DO TUH SPIES ON TH' DESERT!
IF HE ESCAPES HE'LL STARVE TUH DEATH TRYIN' TUH HOOF HIS WAY BACK HERE! AN' IF HE DOES GET BACK, WHADDA WE CARE?
HE'LL BE GONE SO LONG THAT WE'LL HAVE PLENTY O' TIME T' SELL THEM BLUEPRINTS— AN' SCRAM OUT O' TH' COUNTRY!
I'VE GOT A DANGEROUS SPYIN' JOB FER ONE O' YOU MUGS WHO AIN'T AFEARED TUH DIE! WHO'LL VOLUNTEER?
WELL! SPEAK UP!! WHAT ARE YUH— MEN OR MICE?
YOWWWW!
YOU'RE ACCEPTED!
I'M GLAD THERE'S ONE SOLDIER AMONG US THAT'S BRAVE ENOUGH TUH GIVE HIS LIFE FER HIS COUNTRY!
!
!

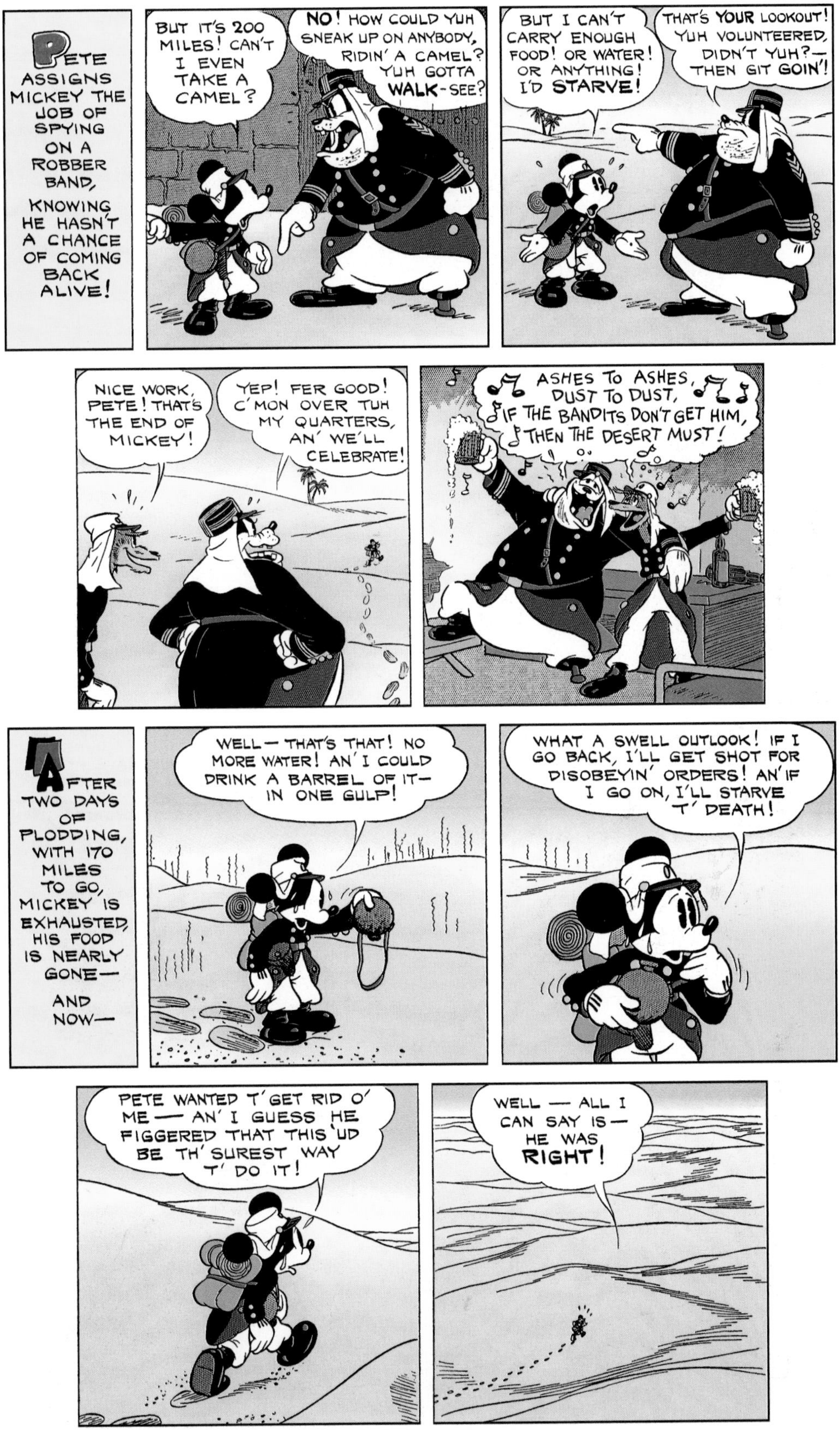
PETE ASSIGNS MICKEY THE JOB OF SPYING ON A ROBBER BAND, KNOWING HE HASN'T A CHANCE OF COMING BACK ALIVE!
BUT IT'S 200 MILES! CAN'T I EVEN TAKE A CAMEL?
NO! HOW COULD YUH SNEAK UP ON ANYBODY, RIDIN' A CAMEL? YUH GOTTA WALK-SEE?
BUT I CAN'T CARRY ENOUGH FOOD! OR WATER! OR ANYTHING! I'D STARVE!
THAT'S YOUR LOOKOUT! YUH VOLUNTEERED, DIDN'T YUH?— THEN GIT GOIN'!
NICE WORK, PETE! THAT'S THE END OF MICKEY!
YEP! FER GOOD! C'MON OVER TUH MY QUARTERS, AN' WE'LL CELEBRATE!
ASHES TO ASHES, DUST TO DUST, IF THE BANDITS DON'T GET HIM, THEN THE DESERT MUST!
AFTER TWO DAYS OF PLODDING, WITH 170 MILES TO GO, MICKEY IS EXHAUSTED, HIS FOOD IS NEARLY GONE— AND NOW—
WELL—THAT'S THAT! NO MORE WATER! AN' I COULD DRINK A BARREL OF IT— IN ONE GULP!
WHAT A SWELL OUTLOOK! IF I GO BACK, I'LL GET SHOT FOR DISOBEYIN' ORDERS! AN' IF I GO ON, I'LL STARVE T' DEATH!
PETE WANTED T' GET RID O' ME— AN' I GUESS HE FIGGERED THAT THIS 'UD BE TH' SUREST WAY T' DO IT!
WELL — ALL I CAN SAY IS— HE WAS RIGHT!

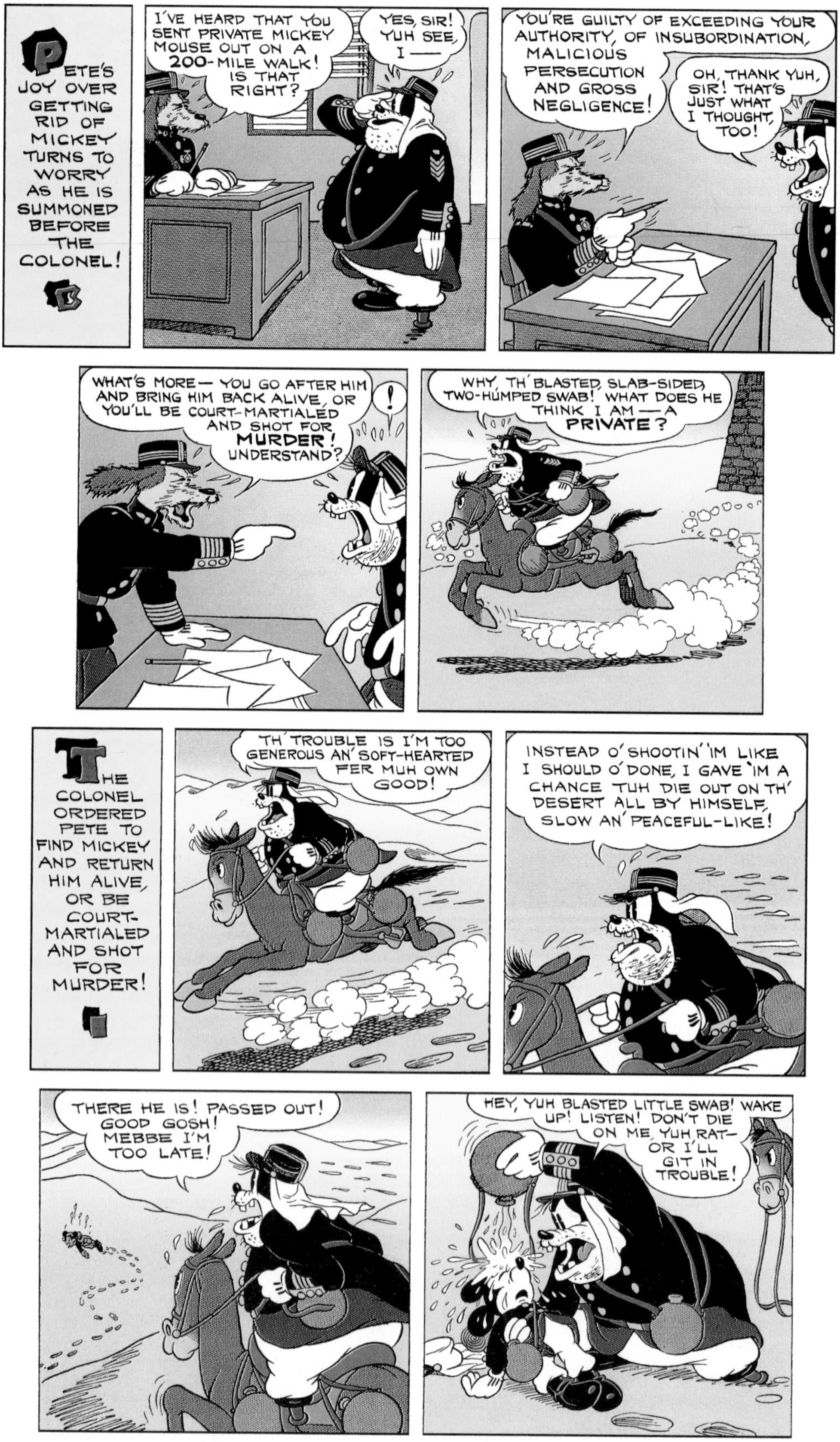
PETE'S JOY OVER GETTING RID OF MICKEY TURNS TO WORRY AS HE IS SUMMONED BEFORE THE COLONEL!
I'VE HEARD THAT YOU SENT PRIVATE MICKEY MOUSE OUT ON A 200-MILE WALK! IS THAT RIGHT?
YES, SIR! YUH SEE, I —
YOU'RE GUILTY OF EXCEEDING YOUR AUTHORITY, OF INSUBORDINATION, MALICIOUS PERSECUTION AND GROSS NEGLIGENCE!
OH, THANK YUH, SIR! THAT'S JUST WHAT I THOUGHT, TOO!
WHAT'S MORE — YOU GO AFTER HIM AND BRING HIM BACK ALIVE, OR YOU'LL BE COURT-MARTIALED AND SHOT FOR MURDER! UNDERSTAND?
!
WHY, TH' BLASTED, SLAB-SIDED, TWO-HUMPED SWAB! WHAT DOES HE THINK I AM — A PRIVATE?
THE COLONEL ORDERED PETE TO FIND MICKEY AND RETURN HIM ALIVE, OR BE COURT-MARTIALED AND SHOT FOR MURDER!
TH' TROUBLE IS I'M TOO GENEROUS AN' SOFT-HEARTED FER MUH OWN GOOD!
INSTEAD O' SHOOTIN' 'IM LIKE I SHOULD O' DONE, I GAVE 'IM A CHANCE TUH DIE OUT ON TH' DESERT ALL BY HIMSELF, SLOW AN' PEACEFUL-LIKE!
THERE HE IS! PASSED OUT! GOOD GOSH! MEBBE I'M TOO LATE!
HEY, YUH BLASTED LITTLE SWAB! WAKE UP! LISTEN! DON'T DIE ON ME, YUH RAT — OR I'LL GIT IN TROUBLE!

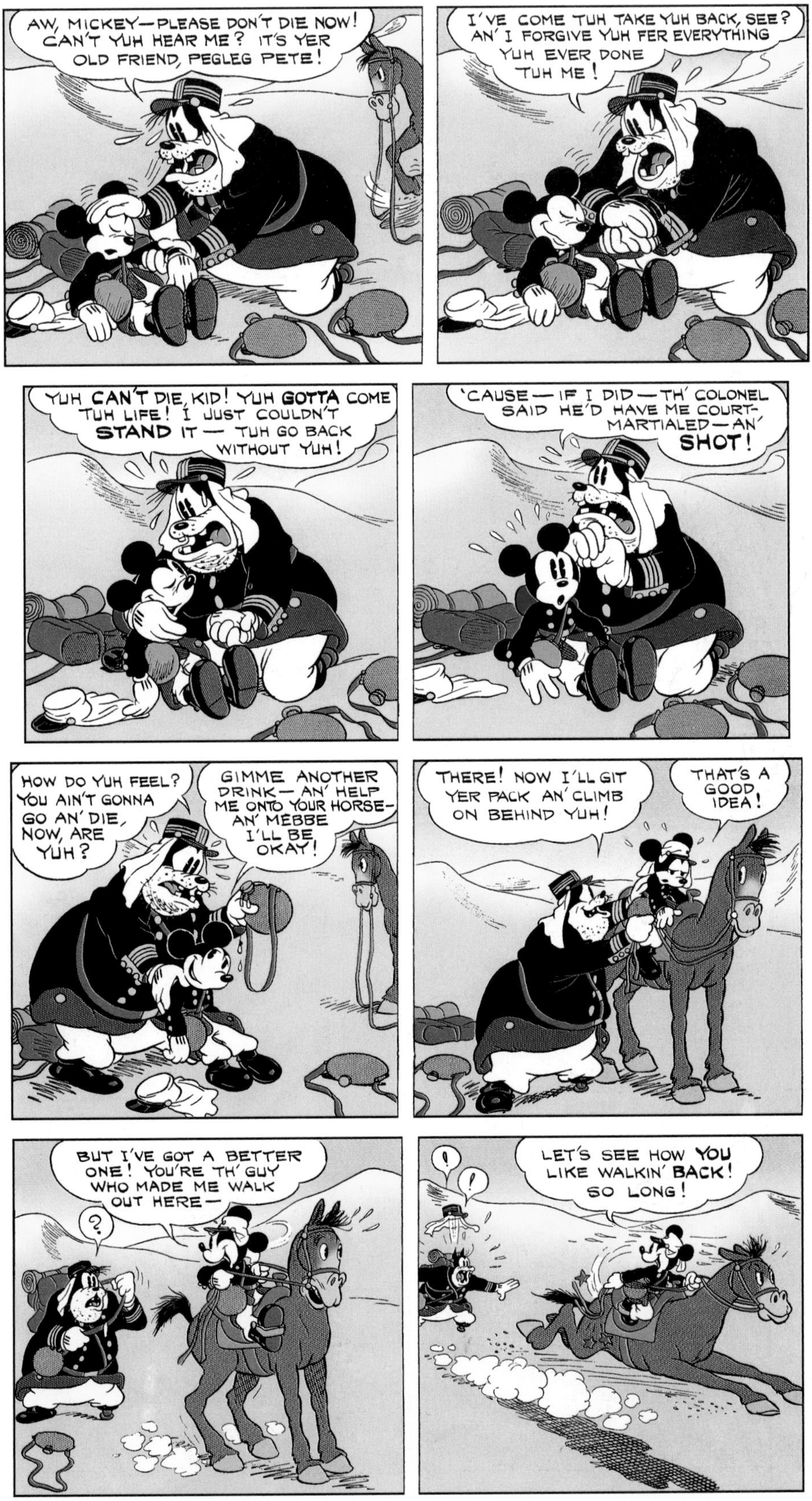
AW, MICKEY—PLEASE DON'T DIE NOW! CAN'T YUH HEAR ME? IT'S YER OLD FRIEND, PEGLEG PETE!
I'VE COME TUH TAKE YUH BACK, SEE? AN' I FORGIVE YUH FER EVERYTHING YUH EVER DONE TUH ME!
YUH CAN'T DIE, KID! YUH GOTTA COME TUH LIFE! I JUST COULDN'T STAND IT — TUH GO BACK WITHOUT YUH!
'CAUSE — IF I DID — TH' COLONEL SAID HE'D HAVE ME COURT-MARTIALED — AN' SHOT!
HOW DO YUH FEEL? YOU AIN'T GONNA GO AN' DIE, NOW, ARE YUH?
GIMME ANOTHER DRINK — AN' HELP ME ONTO YOUR HORSE— AN' MEBBE I'LL BE OKAY!
THERE! NOW I'LL GIT YER PACK AN' CLIMB ON BEHIND YUH!
THAT'S A GOOD IDEA!
BUT I'VE GOT A BETTER ONE! YOU'RE TH' GUY WHO MADE ME WALK OUT HERE—
?
!
!
LET'S SEE HOW YOU LIKE WALKIN' BACK! SO LONG!

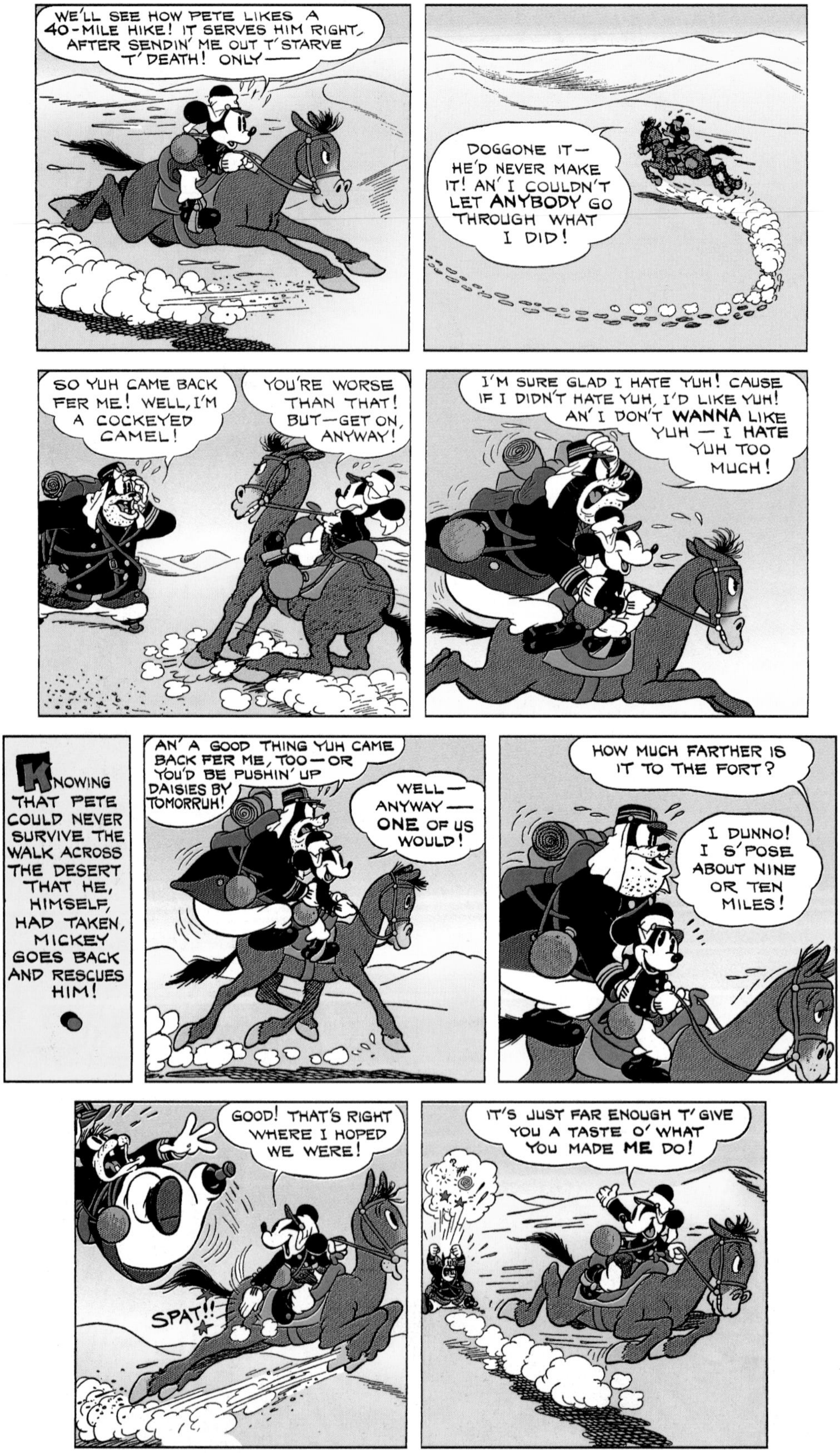
WE'LL SEE HOW PETE LIKES A 40-MILE HIKE! IT SERVES HIM RIGHT, AFTER SENDIN' ME OUT T' STARVE T' DEATH! ONLY——
DOGGONE IT— HE'D NEVER MAKE IT! AN' I COULDN'T LET ANYBODY GO THROUGH WHAT I DID!
SO YUH CAME BACK FER ME! WELL, I'M A COCKEYED CAMEL!
YOU'RE WORSE THAN THAT! BUT—GET ON, ANYWAY!
I'M SURE GLAD I HATE YUH! CAUSE IF I DIDN'T HATE YUH, I'D LIKE YUH! AN' I DON'T WANNA LIKE YUH — I HATE YUH TOO MUCH!
KNOWING THAT PETE COULD NEVER SURVIVE THE WALK ACROSS THE DESERT THAT HE, HIMSELF, HAD TAKEN, MICKEY GOES BACK AND RESCUES HIM!
AN' A GOOD THING YUH CAME BACK FER ME, TOO—OR YOU'D BE PUSHIN' UP DAISIES BY TOMORRUH!
WELL— ANYWAY—— ONE OF US WOULD!
HOW MUCH FARTHER IS IT TO THE FORT?
I DUNNO! I S'POSE ABOUT NINE OR TEN MILES!
GOOD! THAT'S RIGHT WHERE I HOPED WE WERE!
SPAT!!
IT'S JUST FAR ENOUGH T' GIVE YOU A TASTE O' WHAT YOU MADE ME DO!

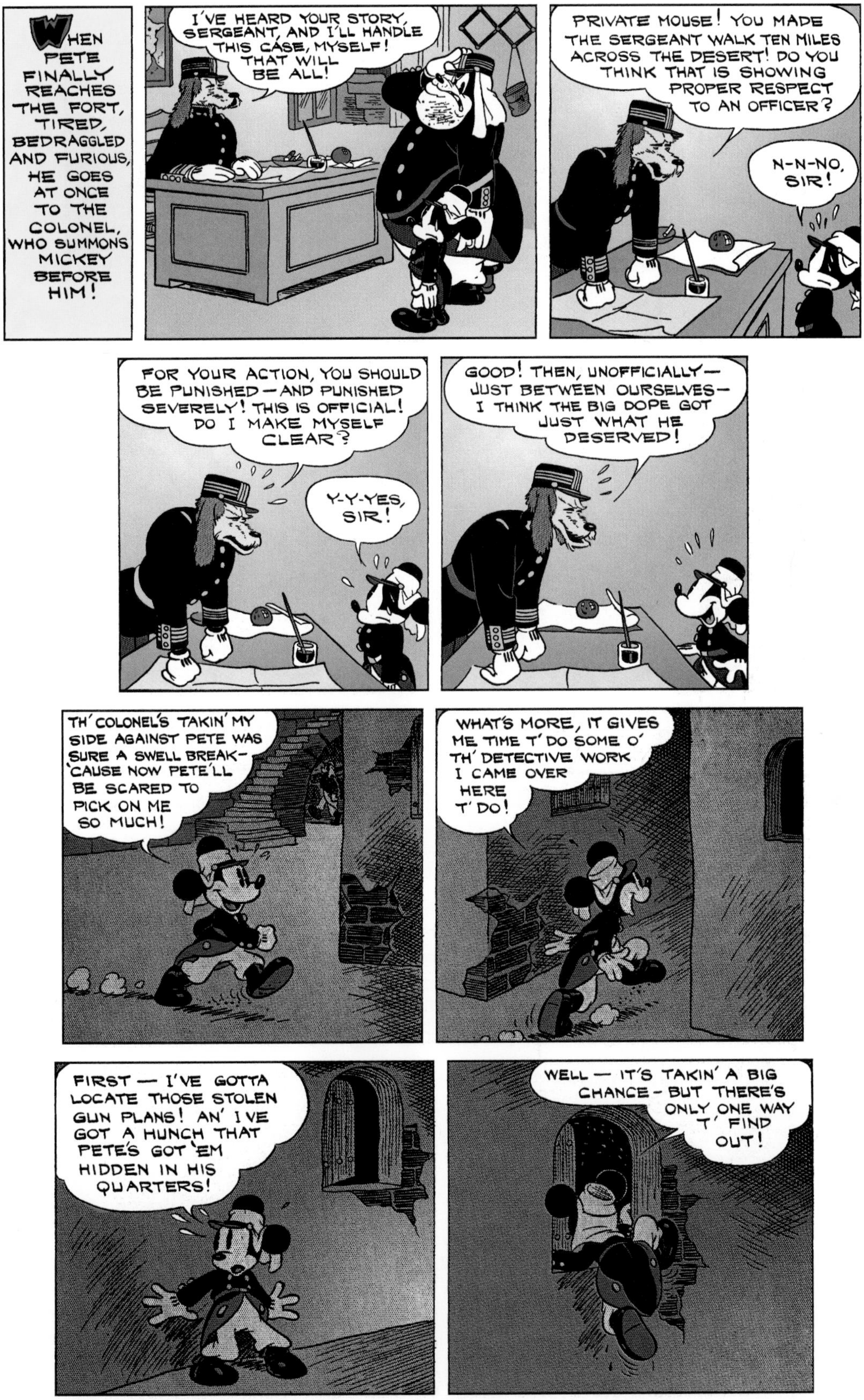
WHEN PETE FINALLY REACHES THE FORT, TIRED, BEDRAGGLED AND FURIOUS, HE GOES AT ONCE TO THE COLONEL, WHO SUMMONS MICKEY BEFORE HIM!
I'VE HEARD YOUR STORY, SERGEANT, AND I'LL HANDLE THIS CASE, MYSELF! THAT WILL BE ALL!
PRIVATE MOUSE! YOU MADE THE SERGEANT WALK TEN MILES ACROSS THE DESERT! DO YOU THINK THAT IS SHOWING PROPER RESPECT TO AN OFFICER?
N-N-NO, SIR!
FOR YOUR ACTION, YOU SHOULD BE PUNISHED—AND PUNISHED SEVERELY! THIS IS OFFICIAL! DO I MAKE MYSELF CLEAR?
Y-Y-YES, SIR!
GOOD! THEN, UNOFFICIALLY—JUST BETWEEN OURSELVES—I THINK THE BIG DOPE GOT JUST WHAT HE DESERVED!
TH' COLONEL'S TAKIN' MY SIDE AGAINST PETE WAS SURE A SWELL BREAK-'CAUSE NOW PETE'LL BE SCARED TO PICK ON ME SO MUCH!
WHAT'S MORE, IT GIVES ME TIME T' DO SOME O' TH' DETECTIVE WORK I CAME OVER HERE T' DO!
FIRST — I'VE GOTTA LOCATE THOSE STOLEN GUN PLANS! AN' I'VE GOT A HUNCH THAT PETE'S GOT 'EM HIDDEN IN HIS QUARTERS!
WELL — IT'S TAKIN' A BIG CHANCE - BUT THERE'S ONLY ONE WAY T' FIND OUT!

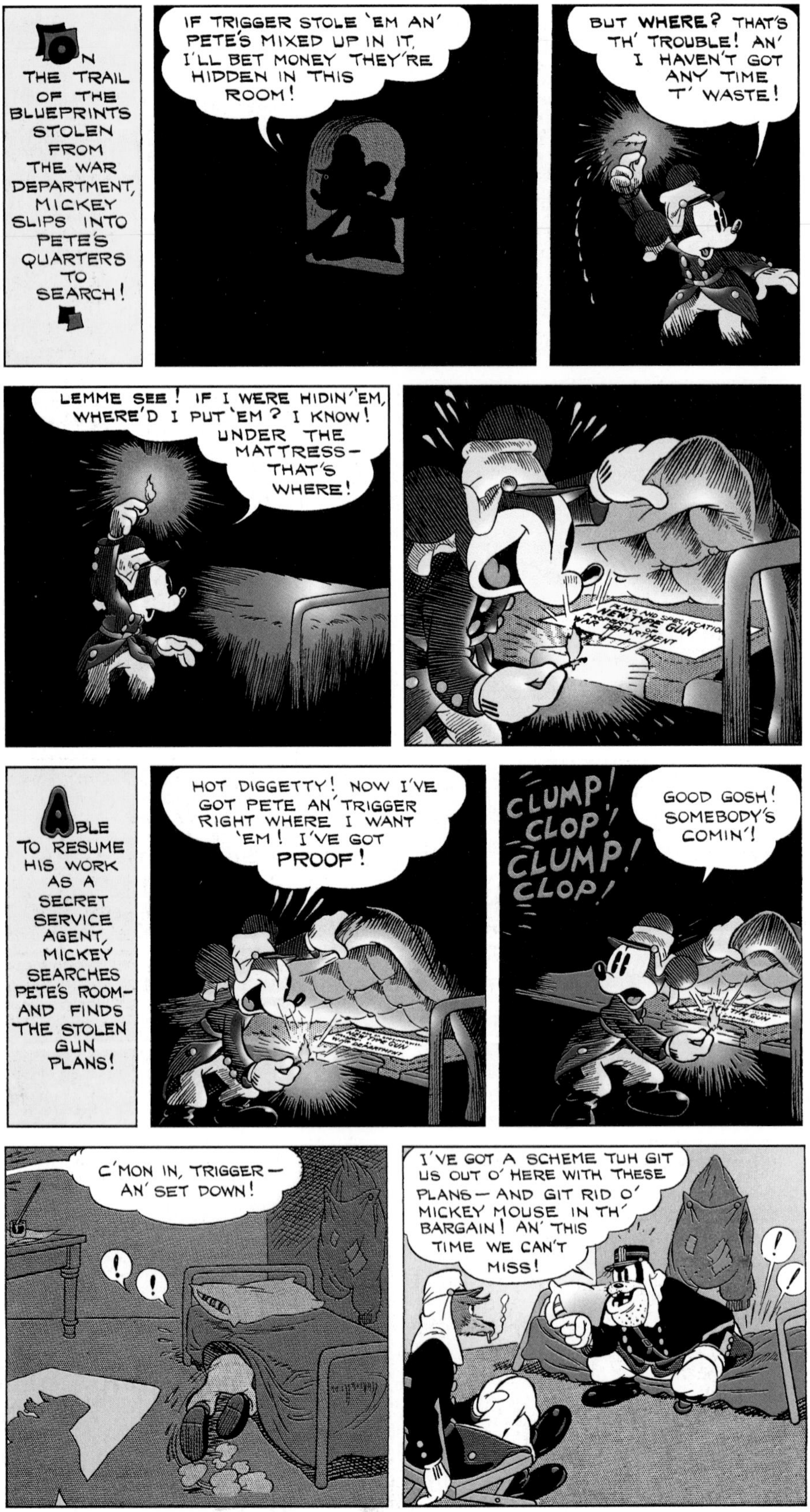
ON THE TRAIL OF THE BLUEPRINTS STOLEN FROM THE WAR DEPARTMENT, MICKEY SLIPS INTO PETE'S QUARTERS TO SEARCH!
IF TRIGGER STOLE 'EM AN' PETE'S MIXED UP IN IT, I'LL BET MONEY THEY'RE HIDDEN IN THIS ROOM!
BUT WHERE? THAT'S TH' TROUBLE! AN' I HAVEN'T GOT ANY TIME T' WASTE!
LEMME SEE! IF I WERE HIDIN' 'EM, WHERE'D I PUT 'EM? I KNOW! UNDER THE MATTRESS— THAT'S WHERE!
PLANS AND SPECIFICATION
NEW TYPE GUN
PROPERTY OF
WAR DEPARTMENT
ABLE TO RESUME HIS WORK AS A SECRET SERVICE AGENT, MICKEY SEARCHES PETE'S ROOM— AND FINDS THE STOLEN GUN PLANS!
HOT DIGGETTY! NOW I'VE GOT PETE AN' TRIGGER RIGHT WHERE I WANT 'EM! I'VE GOT PROOF!
CLUMP! CLOP! CLUMP! CLOP!
GOOD GOSH! SOMEBODY'S COMIN'!
C'MON IN, TRIGGER— AN' SET DOWN!
I'VE GOT A SCHEME TUH GIT US OUT O' HERE WITH THESE PLANS— AND GIT RID O' MICKEY MOUSE IN TH' BARGAIN! AN' THIS TIME WE CAN'T MISS!

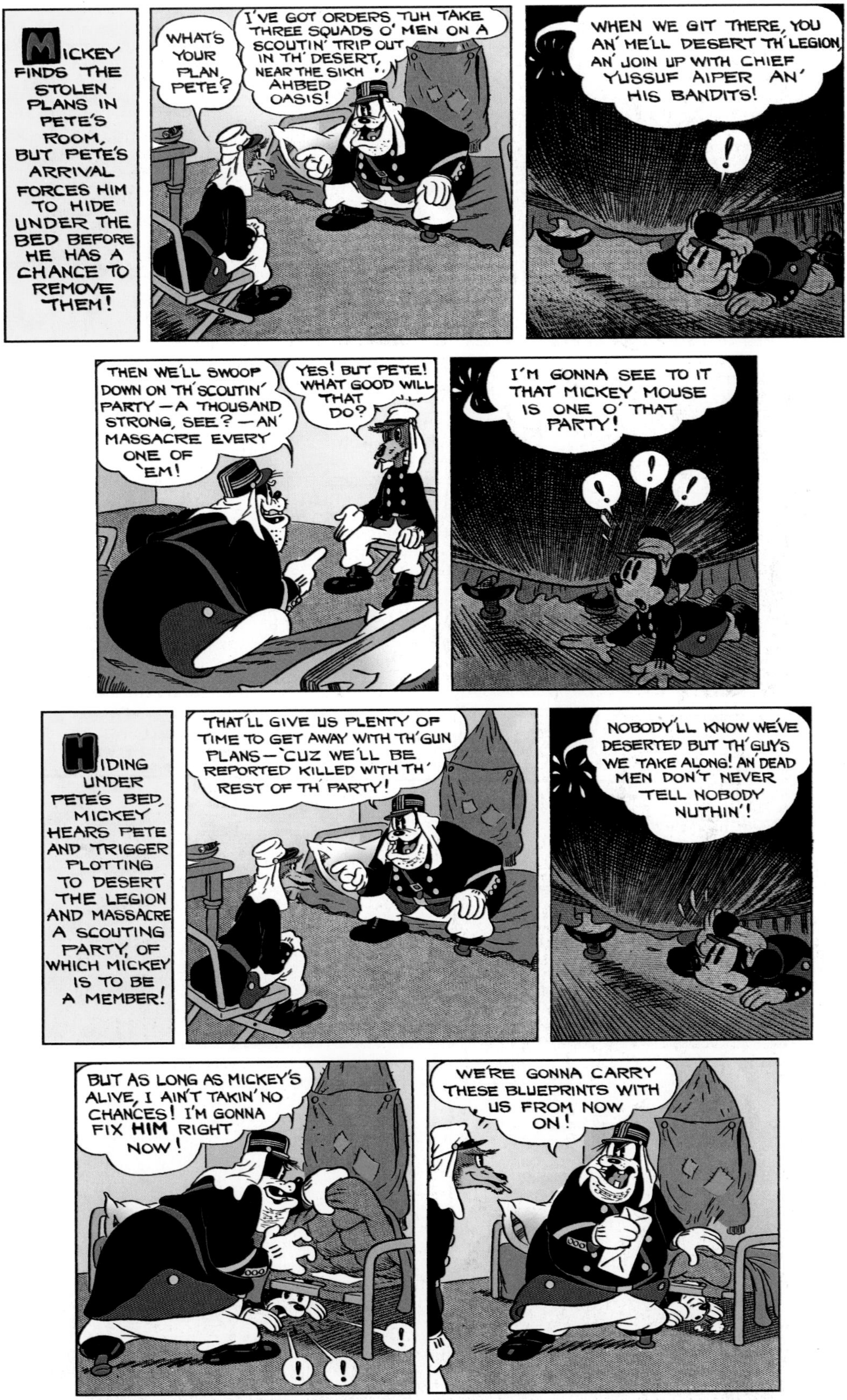
MICKEY FINDS THE STOLEN PLANS IN PETE'S ROOM, BUT PETE'S ARRIVAL FORCES HIM TO HIDE UNDER THE BED BEFORE HE HAS A CHANCE TO REMOVE THEM!
WHAT'S YOUR PLAN, PETE?
I'VE GOT ORDERS TUH TAKE THREE SQUADS O' MEN ON A SCOUTIN' TRIP OUT IN TH' DESERT, NEAR THE SIKH AHBED OASIS!
WHEN WE GIT THERE, YOU AN' ME'LL DESERT TH' LEGION, AN' JOIN UP WITH CHIEF YUSSUF AIPER AN' HIS BANDITS!
!
THEN WE'LL SWOOP DOWN ON TH' SCOUTIN' PARTY — A THOUSAND STRONG, SEE? — AN' MASSACRE EVERY ONE OF 'EM!
YES! BUT PETE! WHAT GOOD WILL THAT DO?
I'M GONNA SEE TO IT THAT MICKEY MOUSE IS ONE O' THAT PARTY!
! ! !
HIDING UNDER PETE'S BED, MICKEY HEARS PETE AND TRIGGER PLOTTING TO DESERT THE LEGION AND MASSACRE A SCOUTING PARTY, OF WHICH MICKEY IS TO BE A MEMBER!
THAT'LL GIVE US PLENTY OF TIME TO GET AWAY WITH TH' GUN PLANS — 'CUZ WE'LL BE REPORTED KILLED WITH TH' REST OF TH' PARTY!
NOBODY'LL KNOW WE'VE DESERTED BUT TH' GUYS WE TAKE ALONG! AN' DEAD MEN DON'T NEVER TELL NOBODY NUTHIN'!
BUT AS LONG AS MICKEY'S ALIVE, I AIN'T TAKIN' NO CHANCES! I'M GONNA FIX **HIM** RIGHT NOW!
! ! !
WE'RE GONNA CARRY THESE BLUEPRINTS WITH US FROM NOW ON!

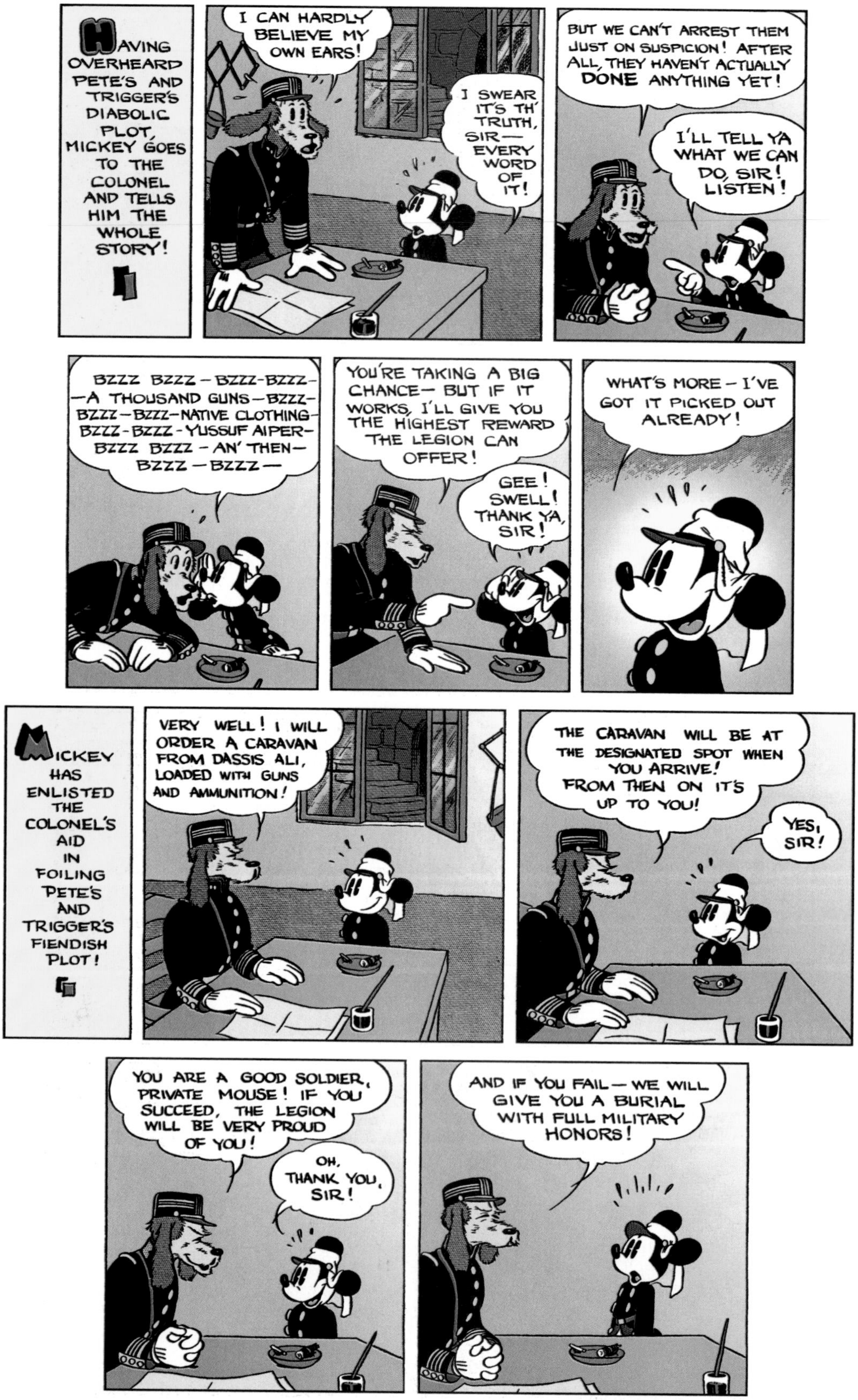
HAVING OVERHEARD PETE'S AND TRIGGER'S DIABOLIC PLOT, MICKEY GOES TO THE COLONEL AND TELLS HIM THE WHOLE STORY!
I CAN HARDLY BELIEVE MY OWN EARS!
I SWEAR IT'S TH' TRUTH, SIR— EVERY WORD OF IT!
BUT WE CAN'T ARREST THEM JUST ON SUSPICION! AFTER ALL, THEY HAVEN'T ACTUALLY DONE ANYTHING YET!
I'LL TELL YA WHAT WE CAN DO, SIR! LISTEN!
BZZZ BZZZ - BZZZ-BZZZ- -A THOUSAND GUNS-BZZZ- BZZZ-BZZZ-NATIVE CLOTHING- BZZZ-BZZZ-YUSSUF AIPER- BZZZ BZZZ - AN' THEN- BZZZ-BZZZ—
YOU'RE TAKING A BIG CHANCE— BUT IF IT WORKS, I'LL GIVE YOU THE HIGHEST REWARD THE LEGION CAN OFFER!
GEE! SWELL! THANK YA, SIR!
WHAT'S MORE - I'VE GOT IT PICKED OUT ALREADY!
MICKEY HAS ENLISTED THE COLONEL'S AID IN FOILING PETE'S AND TRIGGER'S FIENDISH PLOT!
VERY WELL! I WILL ORDER A CARAVAN FROM DASSIS ALI, LOADED WITH GUNS AND AMMUNITION!
THE CARAVAN WILL BE AT THE DESIGNATED SPOT WHEN YOU ARRIVE! FROM THEN ON IT'S UP TO YOU!
YES, SIR!
YOU ARE A GOOD SOLDIER, PRIVATE MOUSE! IF YOU SUCCEED, THE LEGION WILL BE VERY PROUD OF YOU!
OH, THANK YOU, SIR!
AND IF YOU FAIL— WE WILL GIVE YOU A BURIAL WITH FULL MILITARY HONORS!

HELPING MICKEY WITH HIS PLAN TO OUTWIT PETE AND TRIGGER, THE COLONEL GIVES PETE HIS MARCHING ORDERS AS ORIGINALLY SCHEDULED!

I HAVE SENT PRIVATE MICKEY MOUSE ON A GOVERNMENT ERRAND! HE WILL JOIN YOUR PARTY LATER IN THE DESERT!

TAKE THE REST OF THE MEN OUT TO THE SIKH AHBED OASIS, WHERE PRIVATE MOUSE WILL MEET YOU! THAT IS ALL! YOU MAY DEPART AT ONCE!

YES, SIR!

WHILE IN THE NEARBY TOWN OF DASSIS ALI, A STRANGE FIGURE EMERGES FROM THE REAR DOOR OF A CLOTHING SHOP!

Habur Dasha

— — — AND HEADS ACROSS THE DESERT!

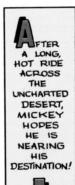

AFTER A LONG, HOT RIDE ACROSS THE UNCHARTED DESERT, MICKEY HOPES HE IS NEARING HIS DESTINATION!

FROM WHAT THE COLONEL TOLD ME, I OUGHTA BE THERE PRETTY SOON! MEBBE THAT MARKSMAN CAN GIVE ME SOME DOPE!

HEY! CAN YOU TELL ME WHERE TO FIND YUSSUF AIPER?

YUSSUF AIPER: ??!!

OH, FER GOSH SAKES

WELL--AT LEAST I SEEM T' BE HEADED IN THE RIGHT DIRECTION!

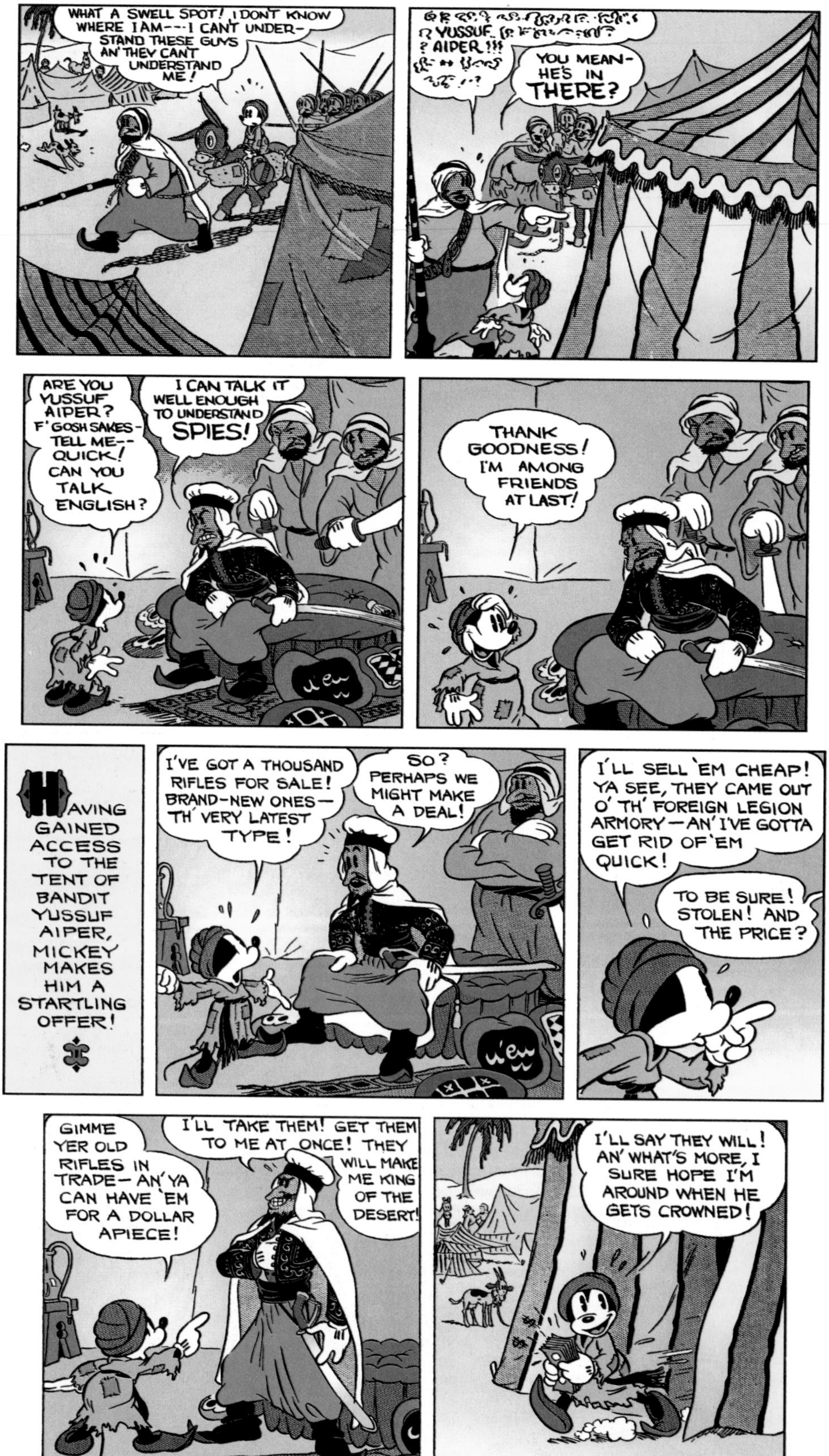
WHAT A SWELL SPOT! I DON'T KNOW WHERE I AM---I CAN'T UNDER-STAND THESE GUYS AN' THEY CAN'T UNDERSTAND ME!
YUSSUF AIPER!!!
YOU MEAN- HE'S IN THERE?
ARE YOU YUSSUF AIPER? F' GOSH SAKES- TELL ME-- QUICK! CAN YOU TALK ENGLISH?
I CAN TALK IT WELL ENOUGH TO UNDERSTAND SPIES!
THANK GOODNESS! I'M AMONG FRIENDS AT LAST!
HAVING GAINED ACCESS TO THE TENT OF BANDIT YUSSUF AIPER, MICKEY MAKES HIM A STARTLING OFFER!
I'VE GOT A THOUSAND RIFLES FOR SALE! BRAND-NEW ONES— TH' VERY LATEST TYPE!
SO? PERHAPS WE MIGHT MAKE A DEAL!
I'LL SELL 'EM CHEAP! YA SEE, THEY CAME OUT O' TH' FOREIGN LEGION ARMORY—AN' I'VE GOTTA GET RID OF 'EM QUICK!
TO BE SURE! STOLEN! AND THE PRICE?
GIMME YER OLD RIFLES IN TRADE—AN' YA CAN HAVE 'EM FOR A DOLLAR APIECE!
I'LL TAKE THEM! GET THEM TO ME AT ONCE! THEY WILL MAKE ME KING OF THE DESERT!
I'LL SAY THEY WILL! AN' WHAT'S MORE, I SURE HOPE I'M AROUND WHEN HE GETS CROWNED!

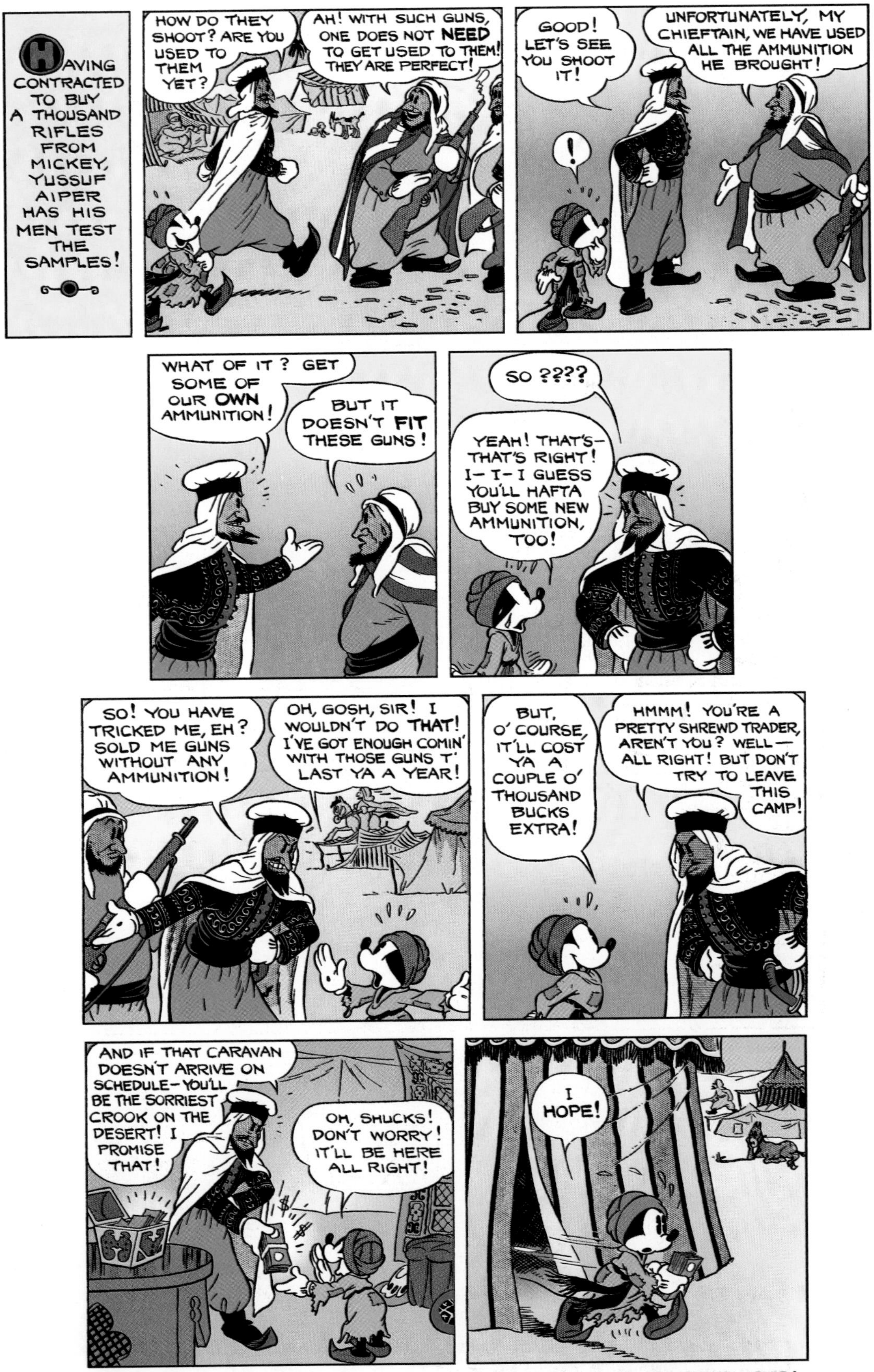
HAVING CONTRACTED TO BUY A THOUSAND RIFLES FROM MICKEY, YUSSUF AIPER HAS HIS MEN TEST THE SAMPLES!
HOW DO THEY SHOOT? ARE YOU USED TO THEM YET?
AH! WITH SUCH GUNS, ONE DOES NOT NEED TO GET USED TO THEM! THEY ARE PERFECT!
GOOD! LET'S SEE YOU SHOOT IT!
UNFORTUNATELY, MY CHIEFTAIN, WE HAVE USED ALL THE AMMUNITION HE BROUGHT!
!
WHAT OF IT? GET SOME OF OUR OWN AMMUNITION!
BUT IT DOESN'T FIT THESE GUNS!
SO ????
YEAH! THAT'S— THAT'S RIGHT! I— I— I GUESS YOU'LL HAFTA BUY SOME NEW AMMUNITION, TOO!
SO! YOU HAVE TRICKED ME, EH? SOLD ME GUNS WITHOUT ANY AMMUNITION!
OH, GOSH, SIR! I WOULDN'T DO THAT! I'VE GOT ENOUGH COMIN' WITH THOSE GUNS T' LAST YA A YEAR!
BUT, O' COURSE, IT'LL COST YA A COUPLE O' THOUSAND BUCKS EXTRA!
HMMM! YOU'RE A PRETTY SHREWD TRADER, AREN'T YOU? WELL— ALL RIGHT! BUT DON'T TRY TO LEAVE THIS CAMP!
AND IF THAT CARAVAN DOESN'T ARRIVE ON SCHEDULE—YOU'LL BE THE SORRIEST CROOK ON THE DESERT! I PROMISE THAT!
OH, SHUCKS! DON'T WORRY! IT'LL BE HERE ALL RIGHT!
I HOPE!

TO BE CONCLUDED!

Walt Disney's Donald Duck in Snow Smitten

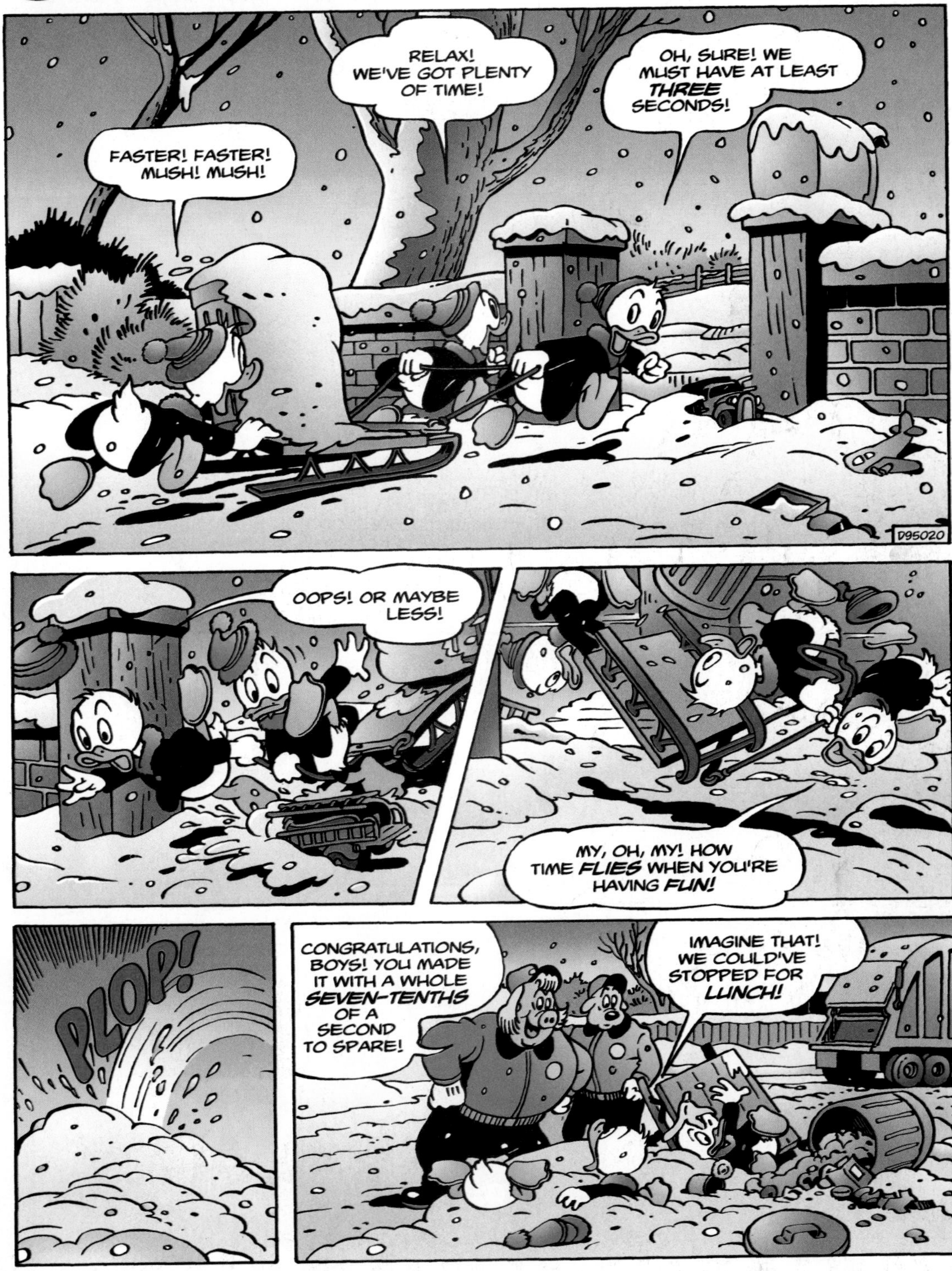

FASTER! FASTER! MUSH! MUSH!
RELAX! WE'VE GOT PLENTY OF TIME!
OH, SURE! WE MUST HAVE AT LEAST THREE SECONDS!
D95020
OOPS! OR MAYBE LESS!
MY, OH, MY! HOW TIME FLIES WHEN YOU'RE HAVING FUN!
PLOP!
CONGRATULATIONS, BOYS! YOU MADE IT WITH A WHOLE SEVEN-TENTHS OF A SECOND TO SPARE!
IMAGINE THAT! WE COULD'VE STOPPED FOR LUNCH!

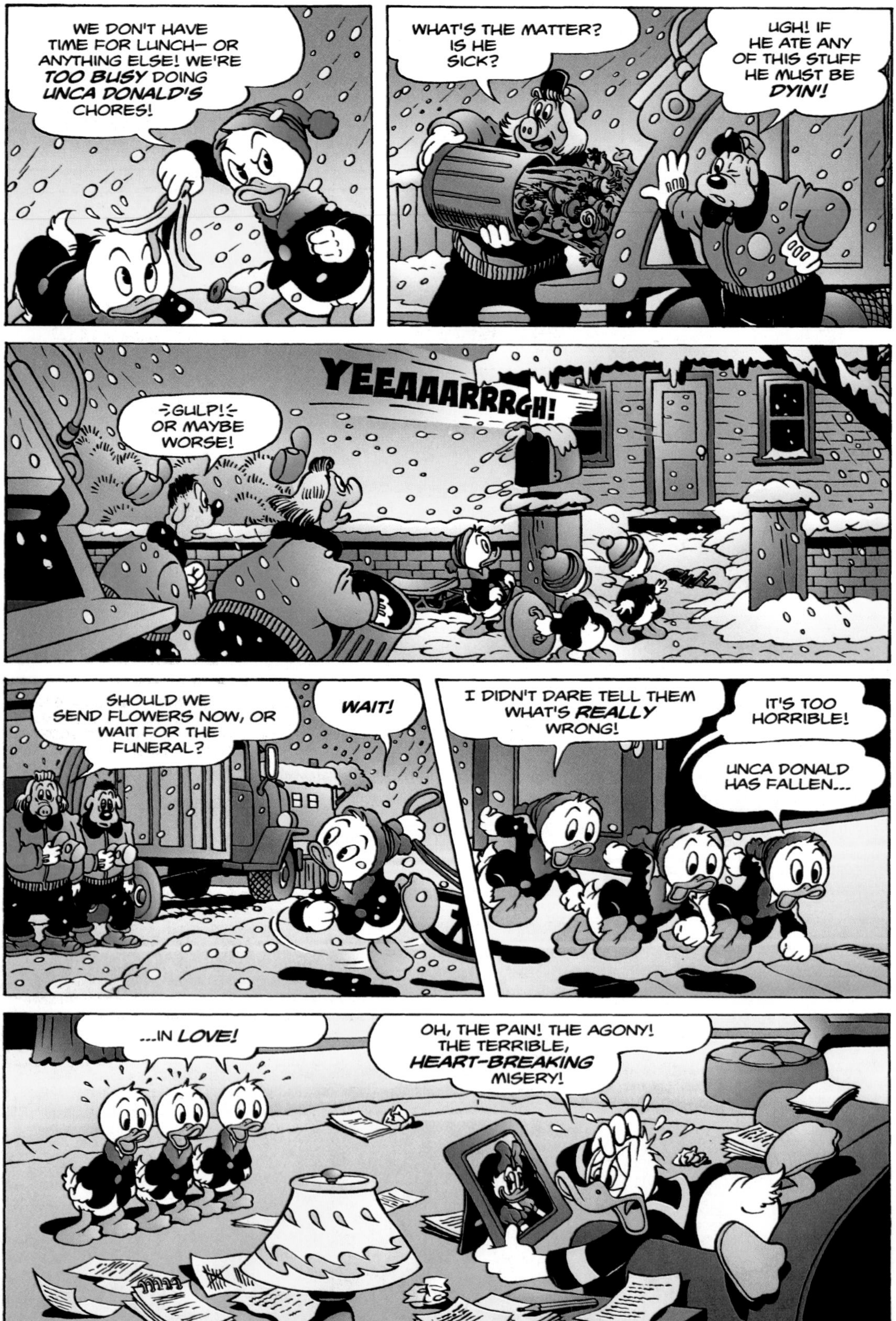
WE DON'T HAVE TIME FOR LUNCH— OR ANYTHING ELSE! WE'RE TOO BUSY DOING UNCA DONALD'S CHORES!
WHAT'S THE MATTER? IS HE SICK?
UGH! IF HE ATE ANY OF THIS STUFF HE MUST BE DYIN'!
GULP! OR MAYBE WORSE!
YEEAAARRRGH!
SHOULD WE SEND FLOWERS NOW, OR WAIT FOR THE FUNERAL?
WAIT!
I DIDN'T DARE TELL THEM WHAT'S REALLY WRONG!
IT'S TOO HORRIBLE!
UNCA DONALD HAS FALLEN...
...IN LOVE!
OH, THE PAIN! THE AGONY! THE TERRIBLE, HEART-BREAKING MISERY!

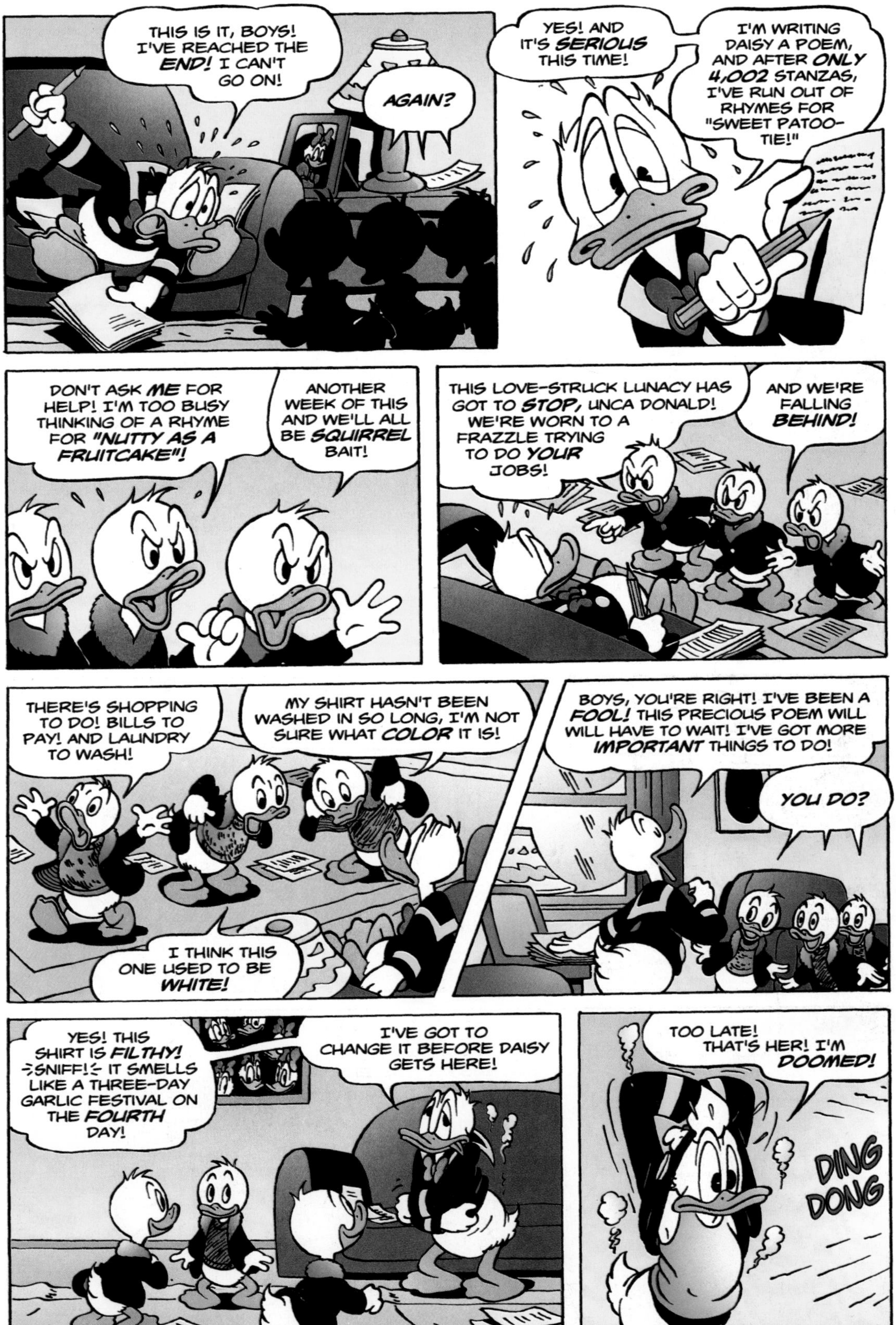
THIS IS IT, BOYS! I'VE REACHED THE END! I CAN'T GO ON!
AGAIN?
YES! AND IT'S SERIOUS THIS TIME!
I'M WRITING DAISY A POEM, AND AFTER ONLY 4,002 STANZAS, I'VE RUN OUT OF RHYMES FOR "SWEET PATOOTIE!"
DON'T ASK ME FOR HELP! I'M TOO BUSY THINKING OF A RHYME FOR "NUTTY AS A FRUITCAKE"!
ANOTHER WEEK OF THIS AND WE'LL ALL BE SQUIRREL BAIT!
THIS LOVE-STRUCK LUNACY HAS GOT TO STOP, UNCA DONALD! WE'RE WORN TO A FRAZZLE TRYING TO DO YOUR JOBS!
AND WE'RE FALLING BEHIND!
THERE'S SHOPPING TO DO! BILLS TO PAY! AND LAUNDRY TO WASH!
MY SHIRT HASN'T BEEN WASHED IN SO LONG, I'M NOT SURE WHAT COLOR IT IS!
I THINK THIS ONE USED TO BE WHITE!
BOYS, YOU'RE RIGHT! I'VE BEEN A FOOL! THIS PRECIOUS POEM WILL WILL HAVE TO WAIT! I'VE GOT MORE IMPORTANT THINGS TO DO!
YOU DO?
YES! THIS SHIRT IS FILTHY! -SNIFF!- IT SMELLS LIKE A THREE-DAY GARLIC FESTIVAL ON THE FOURTH DAY!
I'VE GOT TO CHANGE IT BEFORE DAISY GETS HERE!
TOO LATE! THAT'S HER! I'M DOOMED!
DING DONG

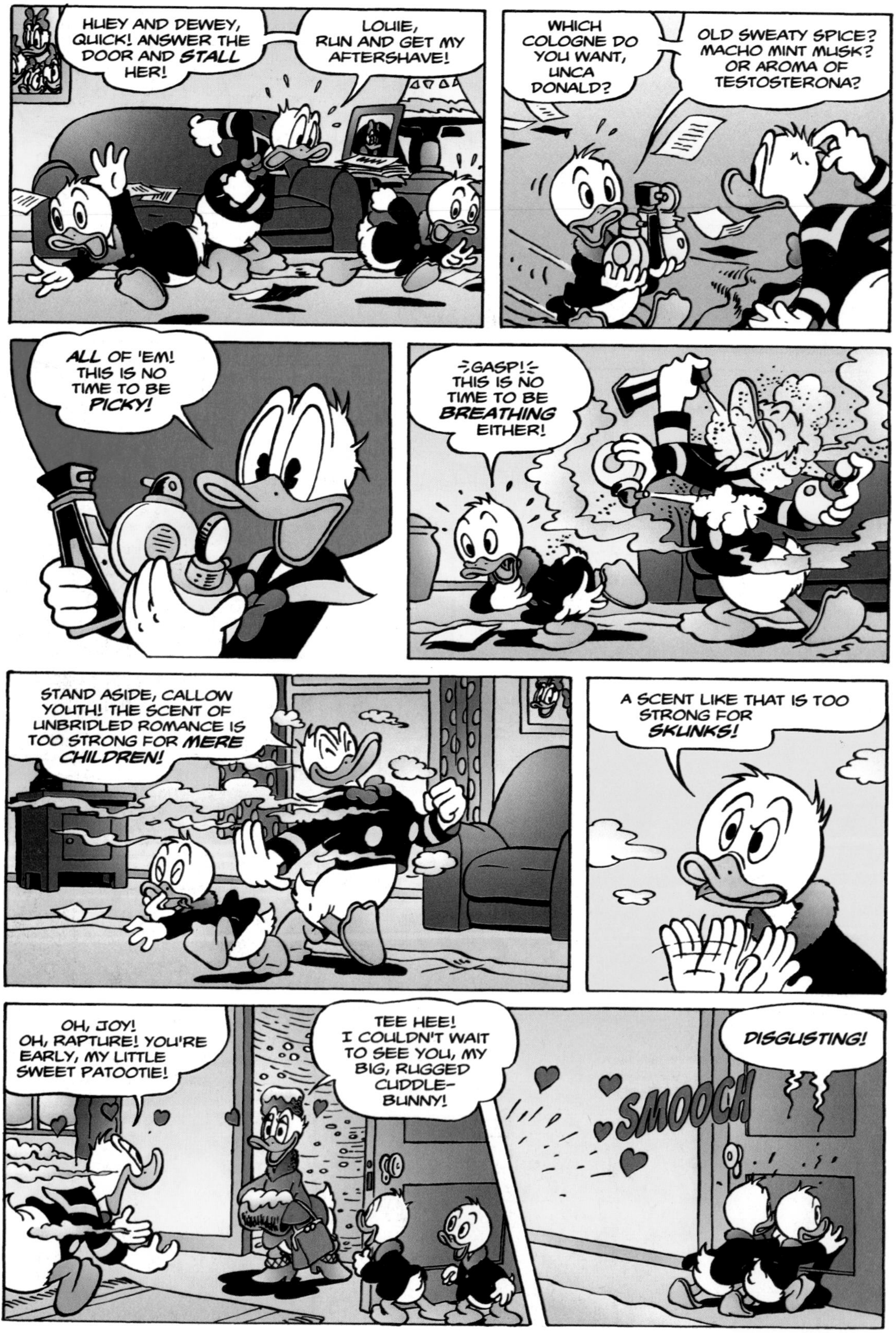
HUEY AND DEWEY, QUICK! ANSWER THE DOOR AND STALL HER!
LOUIE, RUN AND GET MY AFTERSHAVE!
WHICH COLOGNE DO YOU WANT, UNCA DONALD?
OLD SWEATY SPICE? MACHO MINT MUSK? OR AROMA OF TESTOSTERONA?
ALL OF 'EM! THIS IS NO TIME TO BE PICKY!
GASP! THIS IS NO TIME TO BE BREATHING EITHER!
STAND ASIDE, CALLOW YOUTH! THE SCENT OF UNBRIDLED ROMANCE IS TOO STRONG FOR MERE CHILDREN!
A SCENT LIKE THAT IS TOO STRONG FOR SKUNKS!
OH, JOY! OH, RAPTURE! YOU'RE EARLY, MY LITTLE SWEET PATOOTIE!
TEE HEE! I COULDN'T WAIT TO SEE YOU, MY BIG, RUGGED CUDDLE-BUNNY!
SMOOCH
DISGUSTING!

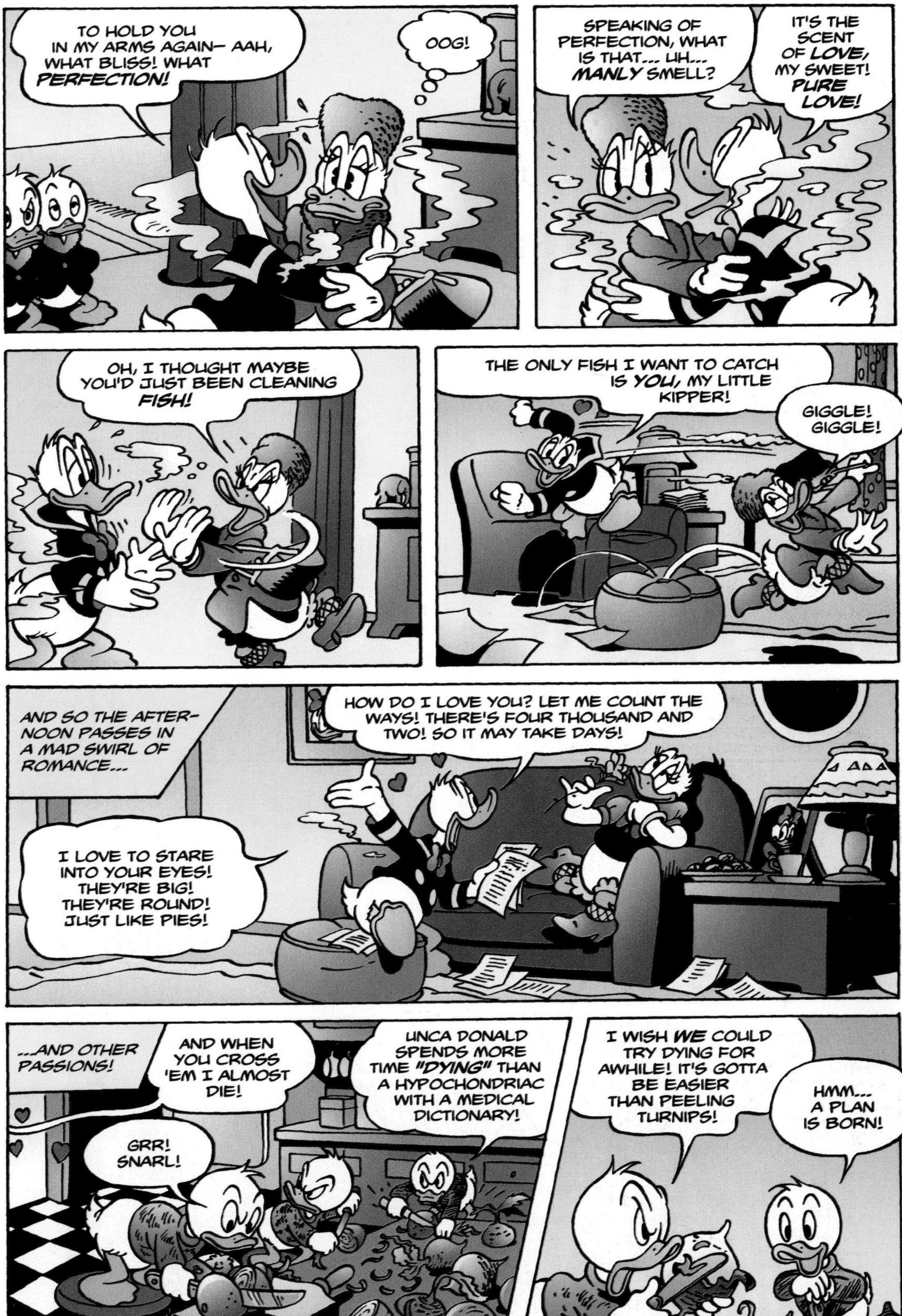
TO HOLD YOU IN MY ARMS AGAIN— AAH, WHAT BLISS! WHAT PERFECTION!
OOG!
SPEAKING OF PERFECTION, WHAT IS THAT... UH... MANLY SMELL?
IT'S THE SCENT OF LOVE, MY SWEET! PURE LOVE!
OH, I THOUGHT MAYBE YOU'D JUST BEEN CLEANING FISH!
THE ONLY FISH I WANT TO CATCH IS YOU, MY LITTLE KIPPER!
GIGGLE! GIGGLE!
AND SO THE AFTERNOON PASSES IN A MAD SWIRL OF ROMANCE...
HOW DO I LOVE YOU? LET ME COUNT THE WAYS! THERE'S FOUR THOUSAND AND TWO! SO IT MAY TAKE DAYS!
I LOVE TO STARE INTO YOUR EYES! THEY'RE BIG! THEY'RE ROUND! JUST LIKE PIES!
...AND OTHER PASSIONS!
AND WHEN YOU CROSS 'EM I ALMOST DIE!
UNCA DONALD SPENDS MORE TIME "DYING" THAN A HYPOCHONDRIAC WITH A MEDICAL DICTIONARY!
GRR! SNARL!
I WISH WE COULD TRY DYING FOR AWHILE! IT'S GOTTA BE EASIER THAN PEELING TURNIPS!
HMM... A PLAN IS BORN!

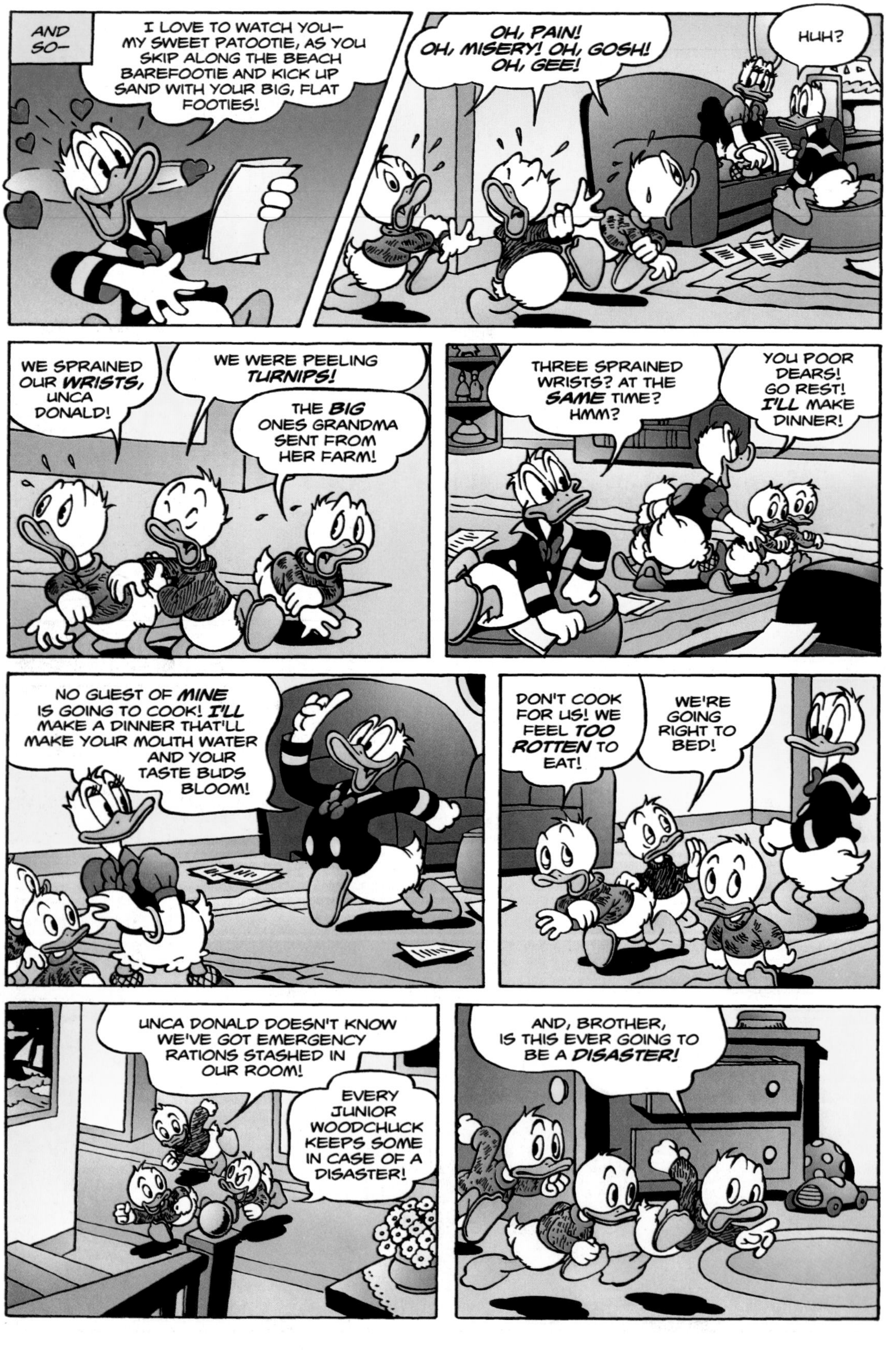
AND SO—
I LOVE TO WATCH YOU— MY SWEET PATOOTIE, AS YOU SKIP ALONG THE BEACH BAREFOOTIE AND KICK UP SAND WITH YOUR BIG, FLAT FOOTIES!
OH, PAIN! OH, MISERY! OH, GOSH! OH, GEE!
HUH?
WE SPRAINED OUR WRISTS, UNCA DONALD!
WE WERE PEELING TURNIPS!
THE BIG ONES GRANDMA SENT FROM HER FARM!
THREE SPRAINED WRISTS? AT THE SAME TIME? HMM?
YOU POOR DEARS! GO REST! I'LL MAKE DINNER!
NO GUEST OF MINE IS GOING TO COOK! I'LL MAKE A DINNER THAT'LL MAKE YOUR MOUTH WATER AND YOUR TASTE BUDS BLOOM!
DON'T COOK FOR US! WE FEEL TOO ROTTEN TO EAT!
WE'RE GOING RIGHT TO BED!
UNCA DONALD DOESN'T KNOW WE'VE GOT EMERGENCY RATIONS STASHED IN OUR ROOM!
EVERY JUNIOR WOODCHUCK KEEPS SOME IN CASE OF A DISASTER!
AND, BROTHER, IS THIS EVER GOING TO BE A DISASTER!

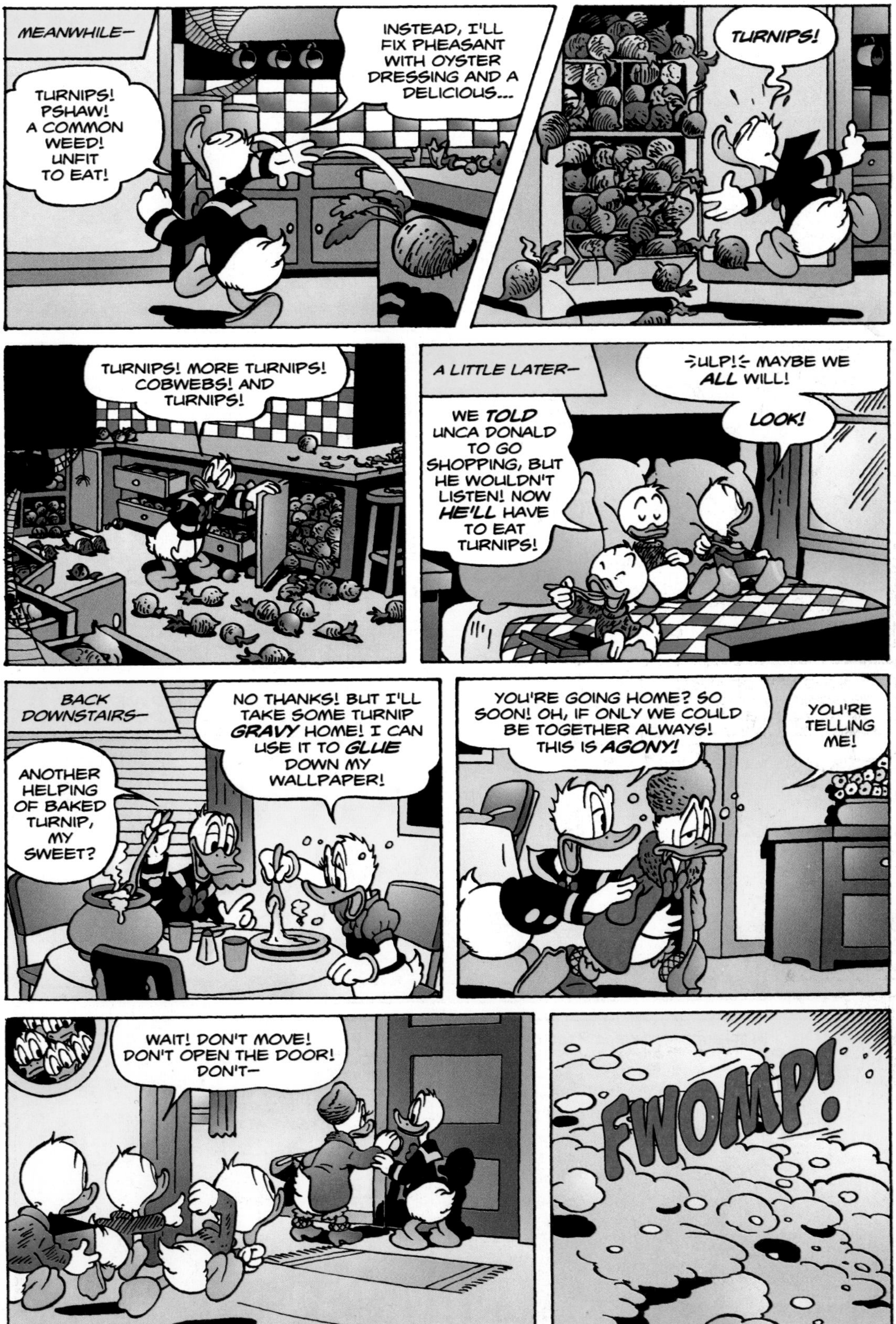
MEANWHILE—
TURNIPS! PSHAW! A COMMON WEED! UNFIT TO EAT!
INSTEAD, I'LL FIX PHEASANT WITH OYSTER DRESSING AND A DELICIOUS...
TURNIPS!
TURNIPS! MORE TURNIPS! COBWEBS! AND TURNIPS!
A LITTLE LATER—
WE TOLD UNCA DONALD TO GO SHOPPING, BUT HE WOULDN'T LISTEN! NOW HE'LL HAVE TO EAT TURNIPS!
GULP! MAYBE WE ALL WILL!
LOOK!
BACK DOWNSTAIRS—
ANOTHER HELPING OF BAKED TURNIP, MY SWEET?
NO THANKS! BUT I'LL TAKE SOME TURNIP GRAVY HOME! I CAN USE IT TO GLUE DOWN MY WALLPAPER!
YOU'RE GOING HOME? SO SOON! OH, IF ONLY WE COULD BE TOGETHER ALWAYS! THIS IS AGONY!
YOU'RE TELLING ME!
WAIT! DON'T MOVE! DON'T OPEN THE DOOR! DON'T—
FWOMP!

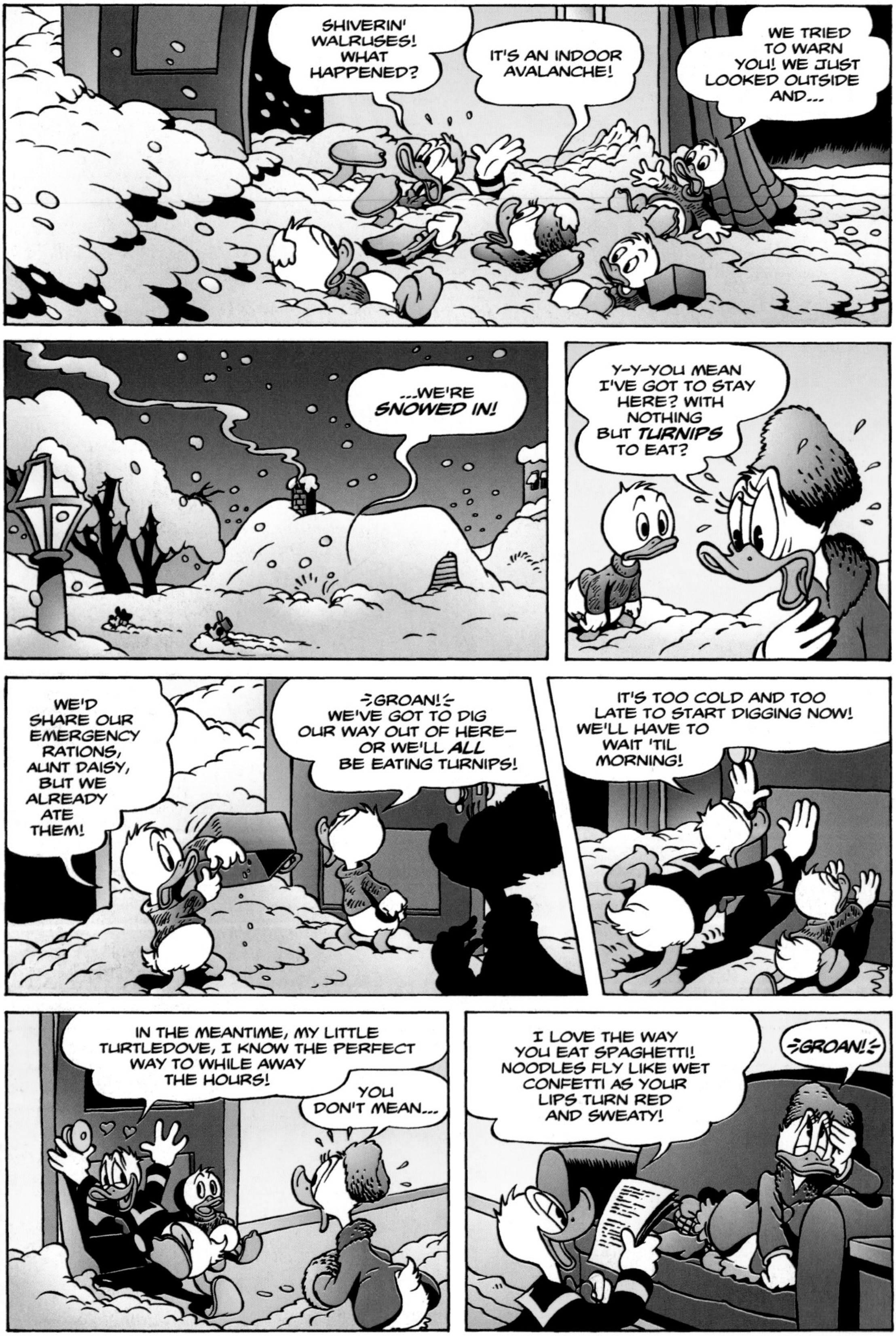
SHIVERIN' WALRUSES! WHAT HAPPENED?
IT'S AN INDOOR AVALANCHE!
WE TRIED TO WARN YOU! WE JUST LOOKED OUTSIDE AND...
...WE'RE SNOWED IN!
Y-Y-YOU MEAN I'VE GOT TO STAY HERE? WITH NOTHING BUT TURNIPS TO EAT?
WE'D SHARE OUR EMERGENCY RATIONS, AUNT DAISY, BUT WE ALREADY ATE THEM!
GROAN! WE'VE GOT TO DIG OUR WAY OUT OF HERE— OR WE'LL ALL BE EATING TURNIPS!
IT'S TOO COLD AND TOO LATE TO START DIGGING NOW! WE'LL HAVE TO WAIT 'TIL MORNING!
IN THE MEANTIME, MY LITTLE TURTLEDOVE, I KNOW THE PERFECT WAY TO WHILE AWAY THE HOURS!
YOU DON'T MEAN...
I LOVE THE WAY YOU EAT SPAGHETTI! NOODLES FLY LIKE WET CONFETTI AS YOUR LIPS TURN RED AND SWEATY!
GROAN!

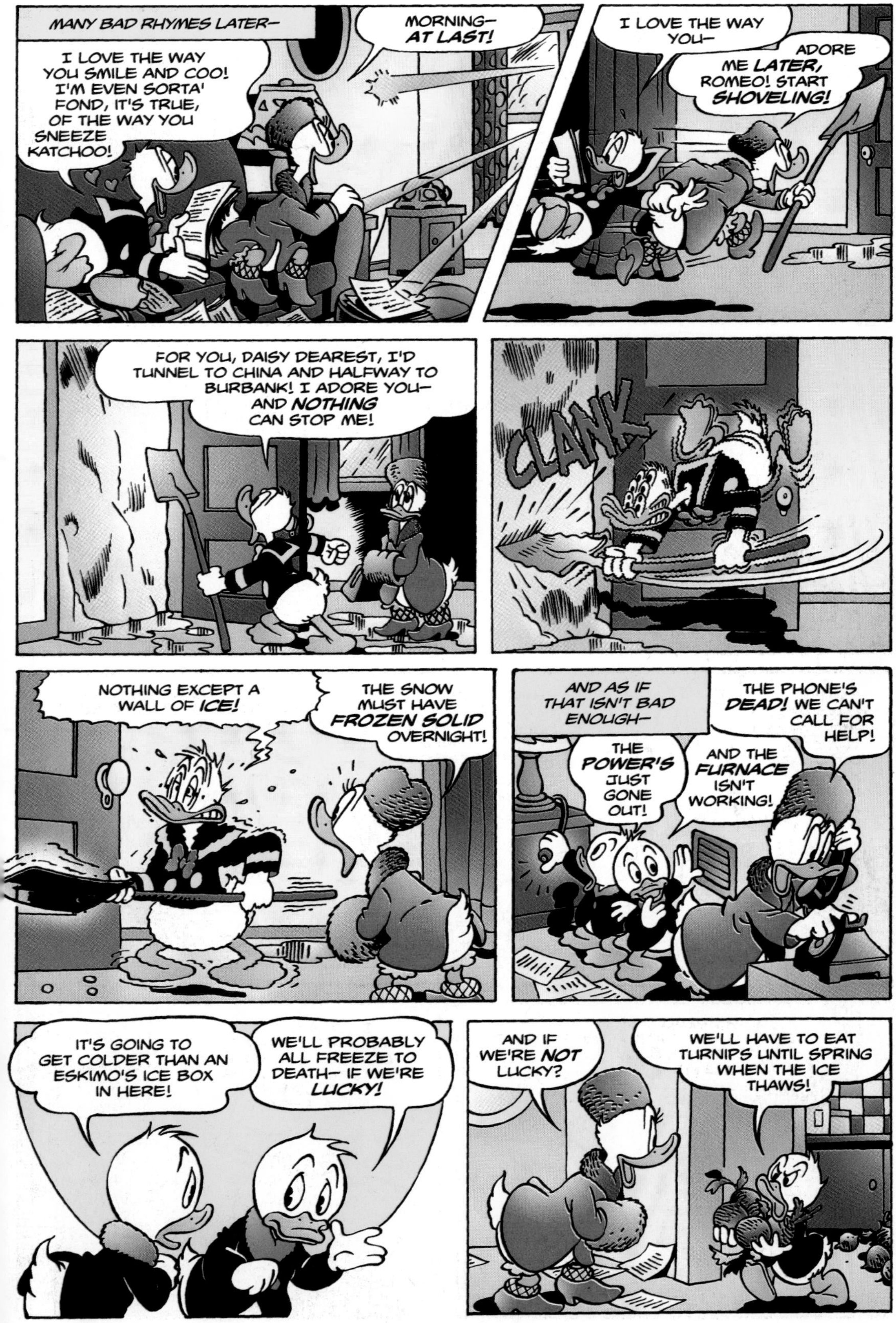
MANY BAD RHYMES LATER—
I LOVE THE WAY YOU SMILE AND COO! I'M EVEN SORTA' FOND, IT'S TRUE, OF THE WAY YOU SNEEZE KATCHOO!
MORNING— AT LAST!
I LOVE THE WAY YOU—
ADORE ME LATER, ROMEO! START SHOVELING!
FOR YOU, DAISY DEAREST, I'D TUNNEL TO CHINA AND HALFWAY TO BURBANK! I ADORE YOU— AND NOTHING CAN STOP ME!
CLANK
NOTHING EXCEPT A WALL OF ICE!
THE SNOW MUST HAVE FROZEN SOLID OVERNIGHT!
AND AS IF THAT ISN'T BAD ENOUGH—
THE PHONE'S DEAD! WE CAN'T CALL FOR HELP!
THE POWER'S JUST GONE OUT!
AND THE FURNACE ISN'T WORKING!
IT'S GOING TO GET COLDER THAN AN ESKIMO'S ICE BOX IN HERE!
WE'LL PROBABLY ALL FREEZE TO DEATH— IF WE'RE LUCKY!
AND IF WE'RE NOT LUCKY?
WE'LL HAVE TO EAT TURNIPS UNTIL SPRING WHEN THE ICE THAWS!

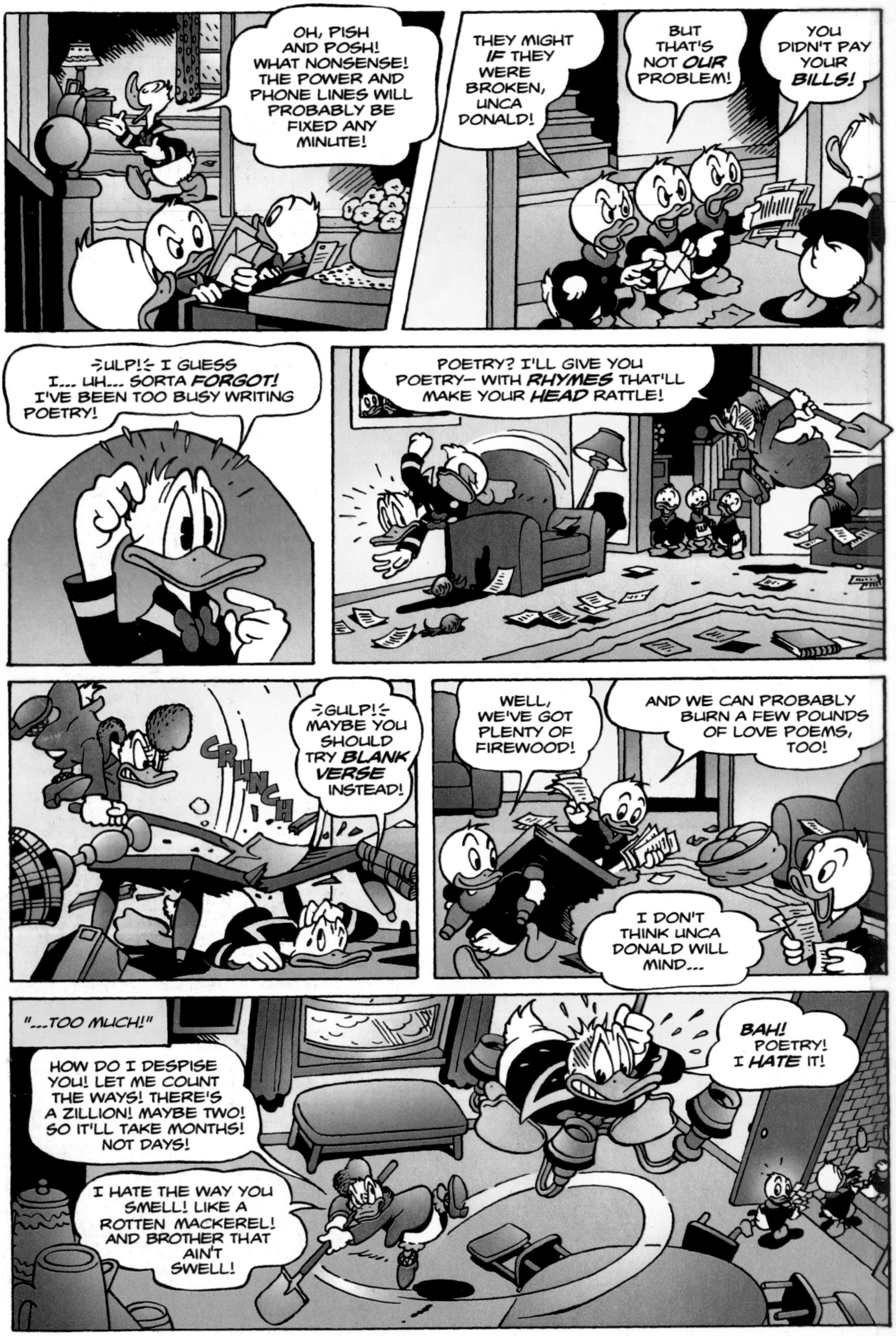
OH, PISH AND POSH! WHAT NONSENSE! THE POWER AND PHONE LINES WILL PROBABLY BE FIXED ANY MINUTE!
THEY MIGHT IF THEY WERE BROKEN, UNCA DONALD!
BUT THAT'S NOT OUR PROBLEM!
YOU DIDN'T PAY YOUR BILLS!
GULP! I GUESS I... UH... SORTA FORGOT! I'VE BEEN TOO BUSY WRITING POETRY!
POETRY? I'LL GIVE YOU POETRY— WITH RHYMES THAT'LL MAKE YOUR HEAD RATTLE!
CRUNCH
GULP! MAYBE YOU SHOULD TRY BLANK VERSE INSTEAD!
WELL, WE'VE GOT PLENTY OF FIREWOOD!
AND WE CAN PROBABLY BURN A FEW POUNDS OF LOVE POEMS, TOO!
I DON'T THINK UNCA DONALD WILL MIND...
"...TOO MUCH!"
HOW DO I DESPISE YOU! LET ME COUNT THE WAYS! THERE'S A ZILLION! MAYBE TWO! SO IT'LL TAKE MONTHS! NOT DAYS!
I HATE THE WAY YOU SMELL! LIKE A ROTTEN MACKEREL! AND BROTHER THAT AIN'T SWELL!
BAH! POETRY! I HATE IT!